W9-BPK-938

EYEWITNESS

VOLCANO & EARTHQUAKE

Lava bomb
Skull from Herculaneum
Sulfur
Gray-Milne seismograph, 1885
Carbonized bread from Pompeii
Cut peridot
Gem-quality olivine
Cut and uncut diamond
Carbonized walnuts from Pompeii
Preserved eggs from Pompeii
Body cast from Pompeii

Pele's hair

Voyager 1 space probe

EYEWITNESS

VOLCANO & EARTHQUAKE

Written by
SUSANNA VAN ROSE

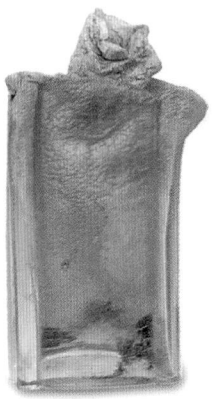

Bottle melted in eruption of Mount Pelée

Perfume bottle melted in eruption of Mount Pelée

Zhang Heng's earthquake detector

Seneca, Roman philosopher who wrote about earthquake of 62 CE

Title page from *Campi Phlegraei*

Fork and pocket watch damaged in eruption of Mount Pelée

LONDON, NEW YORK,
MELBOURNE, MUNICH, and DELHI

Project editor Scott Steedman
Art editor Christian Sévigny
Designer Yaël Freudmann
Managing editor Helen Parker
Managing art editor Julia Harris
Production Louise Barratt
Picture research Kathy Lockley
Special photography James Stevenson
Editorial consultants Professor John Guest and Dr. Robin Adams

RELAUNCH EDITION (DK UK)
Editor Ashwin Khurana
US editor Margaret Parrish
Managing editor Gareth Jones
Managing art editor Philip Letsu
Publisher Andrew Macintyre
Producer, preproduction Nikoleta Parasaki
Senior producer Charlotte Cade
Jacket editor Maud Whatley
Jacket designer Laura Brim
Jacket design development manager Sophia MTT
Publishing director Jonathan Metcalf
Associate publishing director Liz Wheeler
Art director Phil Ormerod

RELAUNCH EDITION (DK INDIA)
Senior editor Neha Gupta
Senior art editor Ranjita Bhattacharji
Senior DTP designer Harish Aggarwal
DTP designer Pawan Kumar
Managing editor Alka Thakur Hazarika
Managing art editor Romi Chakraborty
CTS manager Balwant Singh
Jacket editorial manager Saloni Singh
Jacket designers Suhita Dharamjit, Dhirendra Singh

This Eyewitness ® Guide has been conceived by
Dorling Kindersley Limited and Editions Gallimard

First American Edition, 1992.
This American Edition, 2014
Published in the United States by DK Publishing
4th floor, 345 Hudson Street, New York, New York 10014

14 15 16 17 18 10 9 8 7 6 5 4 3 2 1
001—270656—09/14

Copyright © 1992, © 2002, © 2008, © 2014 Dorling Kindersley Limited
All rights reserved
Without limiting the rights under copyright reserved above, no part of this publication may be reproduced, stored in or introduced into a retrieval system, or transmitted, in any form, or by any means (electronic, mechanical, photocopying, recording, or otherwise), without the prior written permission of both the copyright owner and the above publisher of this book.
Published in Great Britain by Dorling Kindersley Limited.

A catalog record for this book is available from the Library of Congress.
ISBN 978-1-4654-2618-5 (Paperback)
ISBN 978-1-4654-2622-2 (ALB)

DK books are available at special discounts when purchased in bulk for sales promotions, premiums, fund-raising, or educational use. For details, contact:
DK Publishing Special Markets, 345 Hudson Street, New York, New York 10014 or
SpecialSale@dk.com.

Color reproduction by Alta Image Ltd., London, UK
Printed and bound by South China Printing Co. Ltd., China

Discover more at
www.dk.com

Mining transit

Lava stalagmite

Figure of Zhang Heng, Chinese seismologist

Contents

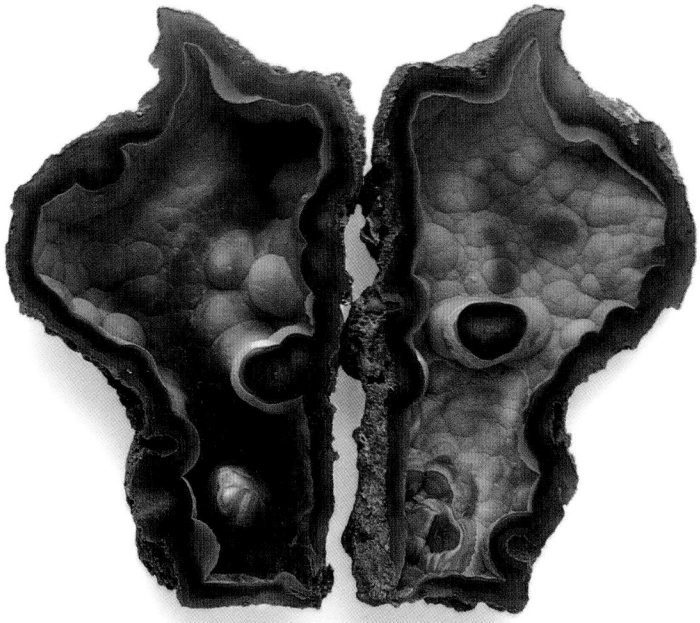

Brown agate

An unstable Earth 6

Fire from below 8

Tectonic plates 10

Mount St. Helens 14

Ash and dust 16

Fiery rocks 18

Gas and lightning 20

Hot spots 22

Ocean floor 24

Mount Vesuvius 26

St. Pierre 32

Affecting the world's weather 34

In hot water 36

Sleeping beauties 38

Life returns 40

Studying volcanoes 42

Other planets 44

When the earth moves 46

Intensity and magnitude 48

Shock waves 50

Measuring earthquakes 52

Mud, fire, and floods 56

State of emergency 58

One step ahead 60

Anger of the gods 62

Did you know? 64

Timeline 66

Find out more 68

Glossary 70

Index 72

An unstable Earth

Volcanoes and earthquakes are nature run wild. An erupting volcano may bleed rivers of red-hot lava or spew great clouds of ash and gas into the sky. During a severe earthquake, the ground can shake so violently that entire cities are reduced to rubble. These natural disasters can be terrifying. But most eruptions and earthquakes cause little damage to people or property.

The perfect volcano
The graceful slopes of Mount Fujiyama in Japan are shown in this print by Katsushika Hokusai (1760–1849). This dormant (sleeping) volcano (pp. 38–39) is an almost perfect cone.

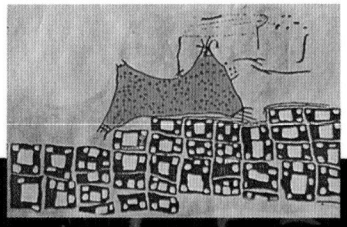

Wall painting
Nearly 8,000 years old, this wall painting is the earliest known picture of a volcano. It shows an eruption of the Hasan Dag volcano in Turkey.

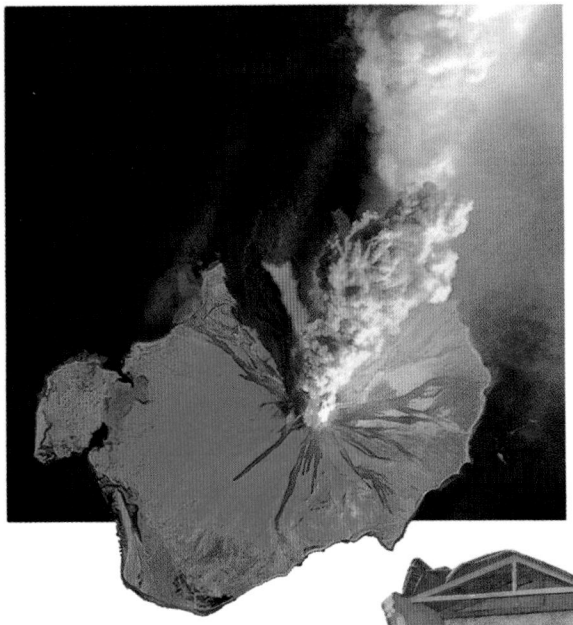

Ash treatment

Volcanic eruptions can have benefits. In Japan, being buried in warm volcanic ash is thought to be good for the health.

Ashy volcano

Observing ashy volcanic eruptions (pp. 14–15) from the ground can be dangerous. This image of the Augustine volcano in Alaska was taken from the safety of a satellite. The ash cloud is being blasted 7 miles (11 km) high.

Old Faithful

Geysers spit boiling water high into the air (pp. 36–37). Old Faithful, an American geyser, has erupted every hour for at least 100 years.

Back from the dead

This painting is of a boy killed during a quake in Assisi, Italy. Legend has it that St. Francis of Assisi brought the boy back to life.

Spitting fire

Mount Etna rises 11,122 ft (3,390 m) over the Italian island of Sicily and is one of the highest and most active volcanoes in Europe. Fountains of gassy lava often spew from the summit (left). The nearby town of Catania is occasionally showered with ash from explosions.

San Francisco, 1989

In 1906, San Francisco was flattened by an enormous earthquake. Earthquakes of this size seem to rock the area every hundred years or so. A smaller quake on October 17, 1989, shook many waterfront houses off their foundations. Some 62 people died in the 15 seconds of shaking.

Fire from below

Deep inside the Earth, rocks melt into a thick liquid called magma (molten rock). Most of the molten rock spewed out by volcanoes comes from the top of the mantle—a layer that lies between the Earth's crust and its outer core. Because magma is hotter and lighter than the surrounding rocks, it rises, melting some of the rocks it passes on the way. If it manages to find a way to the surface, the magma will erupt as lava.

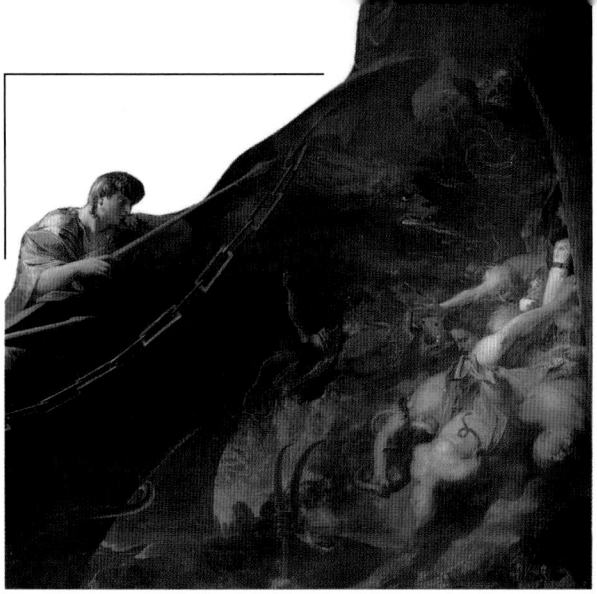

Eternally hot
In Christianity, hell is described as a fiery underworld, as shown in this 1788 painting by Irish artist James Barry.

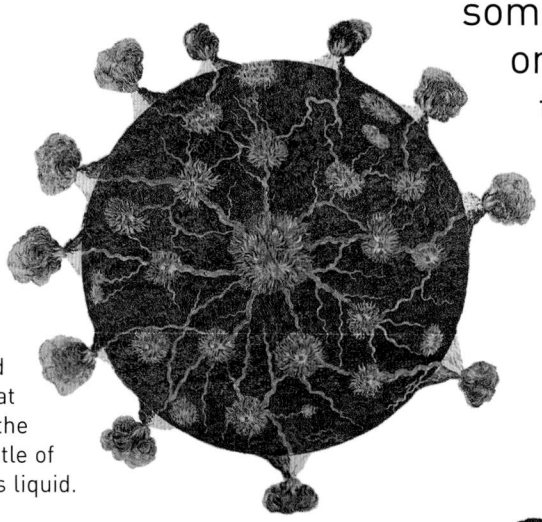

Channels of fire
In this 17th-century engraving, Athanasius Kircher imagined that Earth had a fiery core that fed all the volcanoes on the surface. We now know that little of the planet's interior is liquid.

Red-hot lava (liquid rock) shoots out of a volcano in a curtain of fire

Basalt
The ocean floors that cover three-quarters of the Earth's surface are made of a dark, volcanic rock called basalt.

Into the crater
Jules Verne's famous story *Journey to the Center of the Earth* begins with a perilous descent into the crater of Mount Etna.

Layers of Earth
Just like an apple, the Earth is made up of layers. Its core is surrounded by a moving layer of rock called the mantle. The hard outer layer is known as the crust.

Granite
The continents are made of rocks that are similar to granite—a lighter rock than basalt.

Iron hot

Pure iron melts when it reaches 2,795°F (1,535°C). Most of the Earth is hotter than this.

Iron heart

The iron meteorites that fall to Earth are thought to be pieces of the cores of planets that have broken up.

Lithosphere, which includes tectonic plates (pp. 10–13)

Inner core of solid metal

Upper mantle

Lower mantle

Outer core of liquid metal

Ultramafic nodule

Ultramafic nodule

Inside the Earth

The mantle, lying beneath the Earth's thin, rocky crust, is solid, but it produces pockets of magma that feed volcanoes on the surface. Inside the mantle is the Earth's metal core. This consists of an outer core of liquid metal wrapped around a smaller, solid inner core.

Inner secrets

No drill hole has yet reached as deep down as the mantle. But, occasionally, rising magma breaks off fragments of the mantle on its way to the surface. Known as ultramafic nodules, these fragments of very heavy mantle rock are found in erupted lava flows.

Carrying the weight of the world
In Roman mythology, the god Atlas held the sky on his shoulders. In this statue, he carries the entire globe.

Tectonic plates

Volcanoes and earthquakes are more common in some parts of the world than others. In the 1960s, the secrets of the deep ocean floor began to be revealed. Scientists discovered that the Earth's crust is made up of huge slabs of rock that fit together like odd-shaped paving stones. Called tectonic plates, these chunks of rock move constantly across the surface of the planet at a rate of about an inch a year. Most volcanoes and earthquakes occur at plate boundaries where the tectonic plates collide, rub together, or move apart.

Continental drifter
A German scientist, Alfred Wegener (1880–1930), first used the term "continental drift." He saw the fit of the coastlines of South America and Africa and suggested that they had once been attached. However, his theory that the continents could have moved apart was largely ignored. His ideas were accepted only when spreading ridges (pp. 24–25) were discovered 40 years later.

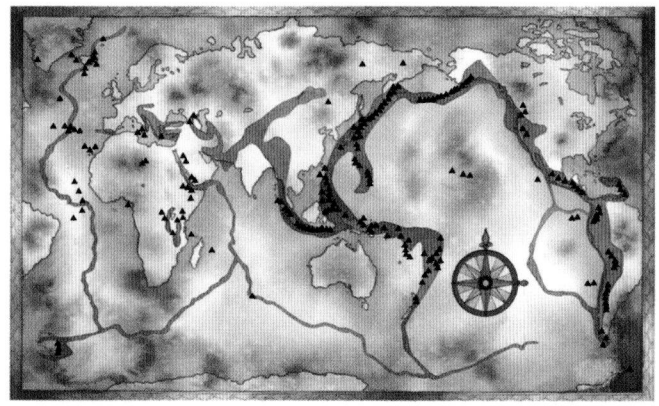

Ring of Fire
The "Ring of Fire" is an area in the Pacific Ocean where most of the world's volcanic and earthquake activity occurs. On this map, the black cones are volcanoes and the red zones are prone to earthquakes.

Lessons of history

This plaster cast shows a man killed in the eruption of Mount Vesuvius, which devastated the Roman towns of Pompeii and Herculaneum in 79 CE (pp. 26–31).

Living on the Ring of Fire

Volcanoes and earthquakes are frequent events in Japan. This huge quake in 1925 damaged the ancient city of Kyoto.

Iceland sits on top of the Mid-Atlantic spreading ridge (pp. 24–25)

Like Japan, Kamchatka is part of the Pacific Ring of Fire

Alaska and the Aleutian Islands have many volcanoes and earthquakes

The Mid-Atlantic Ridge is part of the largest mountain range in the world

The island of Réunion was formed by a hot spot (pp. 22–23) that was under India 30 million years ago

Antarctica is surrounded by new ocean made by spreading ridges (pp. 24–25)

Indonesia, home to over 125 active volcanoes, is at the boundary of two plates

Mount Erebus, an active volcano in Antarctica

Drifting plates

This globe has been colored to highlight the tectonic plates. It is the plates, and not the continents, that are on the move.

There are no active volcanoes in Australia, which sits in the middle of a plate

Fire-land
Iceland is made almost entirely of volcanic rocks like those found on the deep ocean floor. It has gradually built up above sea level through intense and prolonged eruptions.

Moving plates

Most volcanoes are found at plate boundaries, where melting rock forms columns of magma that erupt at the surface. When two plates move apart, a chain of gentle volcanoes, known as a spreading ridge, is formed. Where plates collide, one is forced beneath the other, forming a subduction zone. The sinking plate partly melts and the hot, liquid magma rises. A third kind of volcano erupts above a hot spot, a place where rising magma burns through the Earth's crust.

Ocean floor is older the farther it is from the ridge

Rift (crack) where ocean floor is pulled apart

Old volcanoes that have moved away from hot spot

Hot-spot volcano, builds up a mountain so large it forms an island

30 miles (50 km)

60 miles (100 km)

Magma erupts in the rift as pulled-apart plates release pressure

Hot plume of magma rises to form a hot spot

The new plate cools and thickens as it moves away from the heat of the ridge

Spreading ridges

New ocean floor is made where plates are pulled apart (pp. 24–25), creating a rift (crack in the Earth's crust). Here, magma erupts as lava, creating new rock. All the ocean floor has been made this way in the last 200 million years.

Hot spots

Hot spots (pp. 22–23) are areas in the middle of a tectonic plate, where columns of magma from the mantle rise to the surface and punch a hole in the plate, forming a volcano.

Volcano chain

Guatemala in Central America is home to a chain of volcanoes, many still active. They sit on top of a subduction zone, formed as the Cocos Plate sinks beneath the larger North American Plate.

America's fault

The San Andreas fault is probably the most famous plate boundary in the world. The plates, which constantly slide against each other, move about ½ in (1 cm) a year.

A deep ocean trench is formed where the ocean floor descends in a subduction zone

Continental boundary lifted above subduction zone

There are few volcanoes along transcurrent plate margins

Ocean plate heated as it plunges into the mantle

Lightest melted rock rises through the surrounding dense rocks

Magma reservoir feeds volcano

Lithosphere (crust and very top of mantle)

Asthenosphere (soft, upper part of mantle)

Subduction zone

Where one plate is pushed below another, it sinks into the mantle, partly melting some rocks to form magma. This magma erupts at the surface through volcanoes.

Transcurrent plate margin

Where two plates meet at an odd angle, a boundary called a transcurrent plate margin is formed.

Mount St. Helens

Slumbering giant
Before the eruption, Mount St. Helens had a beautiful, snow-capped peak.

When Mount St. Helens, a volcano in the Cascade Range in the northwestern US, blew its top on May 18, 1980, it had been quiet for 123 years. The massive explosion was heard in Vancouver, Canada, 200 miles (320 km) away. The blast tore off most of the north side of the volcano, leaving a gaping hole. Pyroclastic flows of hot ash and gas (p. 16) rushed down the slopes at terrifying speeds. The explosion continued for nine hours, sending millions of tons of ash 14 miles (22 km) up into the atmosphere. Vast areas of forest were flattened and 57 people were killed.

38 seconds after the first explosion
After two months of small explosions, the north slope of Mount St. Helens suddenly shivered and seemed to turn to liquid. This picture, taken 38 seconds into the explosion, shows the avalanche roaring down the north face and a cloud of ash and gas blasting skywards.

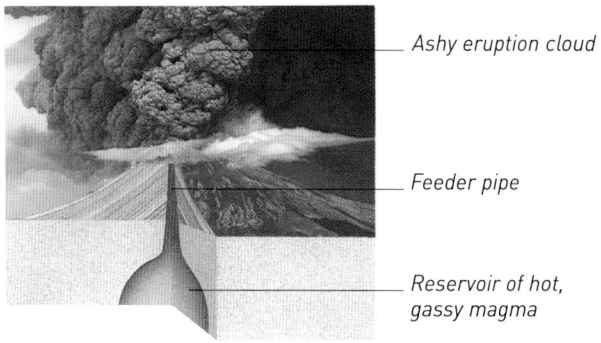

Feeding the fury
Lighter than the solid rock around it, hot magma had risen under Mount St. Helens. It had gathered in an underground pool, called the magma reservoir. The hot rock reached the crater along a feeder pipe.

Four seconds later...
... the avalanche of old rock had been overtaken by the darker, growing cloud of ash, which contained newly erupted material. Gary Rosenquist, who took these pictures from 11 miles (18 km) away, said later that "the sight... was so overwhelming that I became dizzy and had to turn away to keep my balance."

Moving wall of ash

As the ash cloud blasted out, it became lighter than air and began to rise. Gary Rosenquist took this picture before he ran for his car. "The turbulent cloud loomed behind us as we sped down Road 99," he wrote later. "Mudballs flattened against the windshield. Minutes later it was completely dark."

Last gasp

In the months after the eruption, thick, sticky lava was squeezed from the magma reservoir like toothpaste from a tube. It formed a bulging dome, which reached a height of 853 ft (260 m) in 1986. The dome later crumbled into lava fragments.

Flattened forests

Mature forests of trees up to 165 ft (50 m) tall were uprooted by the blast of the eruption.

Eleven seconds later...

... the avalanche of old rock had been completely overtaken by the faster blast of ash. On the right, huge chunks of rock could be seen as they were catapulted out of the cloud.

Ash and dust

Explosive volcanoes pour clouds of ash into the sky. The ash is formed from volcanic rock that has been blown into billions of tiny pieces. These rock fragments, known as pyroclastics, range from huge lava blocks (p. 18) to fine, powdery dust (pp. 34–35). Between these two extremes are lapilli (Latin for "little stones") and ash. Sometimes the ash clouds collapse under their own weight, forming pyroclastic flows or surges. Unlike lava flows, pyroclastic flows can be extremely dangerous.

Lapilli, bite-sized fragments of frothy lava

Ash, smaller pyroclastic fragments

Dust, the smallest and lightest lava fragments

Constructing a cone

Mountains are built up as pyroclastic fragments settle in layers on a volcano's slopes. Gassy fire-fountain eruptions build cinder cones of bombs and ash.

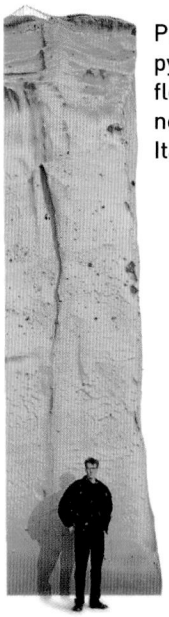

Prehistoric pyroclastic flow deposit, near Naples, Italy

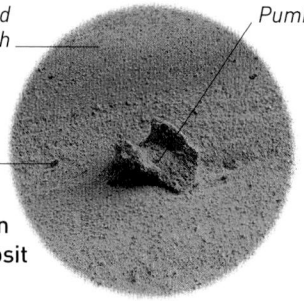

Detail of Neapolitan pyroclastic flow deposit

Glowing avalanches

If the erupted mixture of hot rocks and gas is heavier than air, it can flow downhill at more than 60 mph (100 kph). Such a pyroclastic flow will flatten everything in its path. Equally destructive are pyroclastic surges—flows that contain more hot gas than ash.

Volcano biography

Frozen in a volcano's slopes is a record of its past eruptions. The rock layers can be dated and their textures analyzed. The ash layers in this rock (right) erupted from a volcano about 500 million years ago.

Their fields buried in ash, farmers take their buffalo and head for greener pastures

Night of the ash cloud

After lying dormant for 600 years, Mount Pinatubo in the Philippines began erupting in June 1991. Huge clouds of ash were thrown into the air, blocking out the sunlight for days. Over 300 ft (100 m) of ash lay on the upper slopes of the volcano. Torrential rains followed, causing mud flows that swept away roads, bridges, and several villages (p. 56). At least 400 people were killed and another 400,000 were left homeless.

Buried crops
A thin fall of ash fertilizes the soil (pp. 40–41), but too much destroys crops. Whole harvests were lost in the heavy ash falls that followed the eruptions of Mount Pinatubo.

Taking a breath
Every step raises fine ash that fills the air. Covering the mouth and nose with a wet cloth helps to keep the throat and lungs clear.

Fiery rocks

Volcanoes spew out red-hot lava. Sometimes the lava oozes gently from a hole in the ground. At other times it is hurled into the air in spectacular fire fountains. When it lands, the lava flows down in rivers of hot rock that can cover the countryside. If the lava is less fluid, explosions may occur as volcanic gas escapes from the hot rock. These explosions throw out chunks of flying lava, known as bombs and blocks.

Reheated lava
Some of the gas dissolved in lava is lost when it cools. This piece of lava frothed up when it was reheated, showing that it still contained a lot of its original gas.

Bomb thrown out by Mount Etna on the island of Sicily in Italy (pp. 6–7)

Small, explosive eruption photographed at night on Mount Etna

Dense, round bomb

Bombs and blocks
Bombs and blocks can be as big as houses or as small as tennis balls. Bombs are usually more rounded, while blocks are more dense and angular. Their shapes depend upon how fluid or gassy the lava was during the eruption.

Twisted tail
The odd twists and tails of many bombs are formed as they spin through the air.

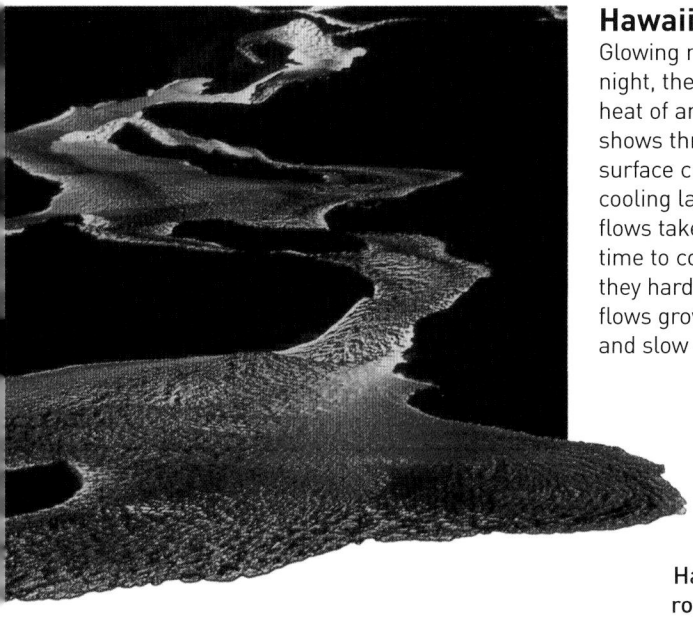

Hawaiian aa

Glowing red at night, the intense heat of an aa flow shows through the surface crust of cooling lava. Lava flows take a long time to cool. As they harden, the flows grow thicker and slow down.

Hardened chunk of ropy pahoehoe lava

Pahoehoe flows

Pahoehoe is more fluid than aa and contains more gas. As its surface cools, the flow grows a thin skin. The hot lava on the inside makes the skin wrinkle so its surface looks like the coils of a rope. The crust may grow so thick that people can walk across it while red-hot lava continues to flow in a tunnel below (p. 23).

Aa and pahoehoe flows

Lava flows pose little danger to people because they rarely travel faster than a few miles an hour. The two kinds of flows get their names from Hawaiian words. Aa (pronounced *ah-ah*) flows are covered in sharp, angular chunks of lava known as scoria. Pahoehoe (*pa-hoy-hoy*) flows grow a smooth skin soon after they leave the vent.

Spiny and twisted

This chunk of scoria from the surface of an aa flow was twisted as it was carried along.

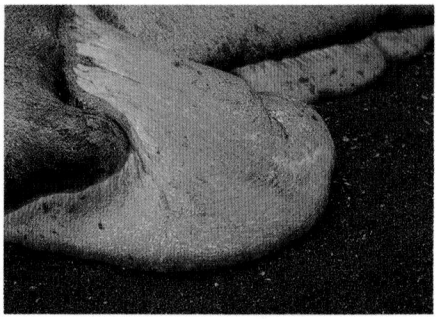

Pahoehoe toe

This picture shows red-hot pahoehoe bulging through a crack in its own skin. New skin is forming over the bulge. A pahoehoe flow creeps forward with thousands of little breakouts like this one.

Driblets of remelted lava from the roof of a pahoehoe tunnel

Black sand from the volcanic island of Santorini, Greece

Fire and water

Volcanic islands like Hawaii are usually fringed by black beaches. The sand is formed when hot lava hits the sea and is shattered into tiny particles. It is black because the lava is rich in dark minerals.

Gas and lightning

Captain Haddock and friends flee from a volcano's gases in the Tintin adventure *Flight 714*

Volcanic gases are extremely dangerous. In August 1986, an explosion in Lake Nyos in Cameroon, Africa, released a cloud of volcanic gases. The poisonous fumes killed 1,700 people living in villages nearby. The main killer was carbon dioxide, which has no odor and is very hard to detect. Volcanic gases, on the other hand, are extremely smelly; hydrogen sulfide, for example, smells like rotten cabbage, and the acid gases hydrogen chloride and sulfur dioxide sting the eyes and throat. They also eat through clothes, leaving holes with bleached haloes around them.

Raising a stink
Nearly 40 years after the last eruption of Kawah Idjen in Java, Indonesia, sulfur and other gases are still escaping into the volcano's crater.

Steam-assisted eruption
When the new island of Surtsey was formed off Iceland in 1963 (p.41), seawater poured into the volcano's vent and hit the hot magma, producing spectacular explosions and huge clouds of steam.

Gas mask
Made to protect the wearer against low concentrations of acid gases, this gas mask also keeps out all but the finest volcanic dust.

Volcanologist studying Hawaiian lava flows behind the safety of a gas mask

Lightning flash

Immense flashes of lightning are often seen during eruptions. They are caused by a buildup of static electricity produced when tiny fragments of lava in an ash cloud rub against each other. This picture shows lightning bolts at Mount Tolbachik in Siberia. It was taken during the day—the Sun can be seen on the left, shining through a cloud of dust and gas.

Vesuvius

Lord Hamilton, British ambassador to Naples, saw lightning flashes as he watched the 1779 eruption of Vesuvius (p. 31).

Floating on an acid lake

Volcanologists sample volcanic gases from an acid lake in the crater of Kawah Idjen. The gases rising from the volcano are dissolved in the lake water that fills much of the crater. Such acid lakes are very hostile to life and would burn a swimmer's skin in minutes.

Floating rock

The volcanic rock pumice is light because it is full of bubbles of gas. Some pumice is light enough to float on water.

Hot spots

The largest volcanoes on Earth are found above hot spots—areas deep within the Earth's mantle that produce huge volumes of magma. When the hot magma rises, it burns through the Earth's crust, creating a volcano (pp. 12–13). Many volcanic islands, such as Iceland and Hawaii, are located above hot spots. The Hawaiian island chain is part of a huge undersea mountain range that formed over millions of years as the hot spot erupted great volumes of lava onto the moving plate above it.

Mauna Loa erupts
Two of the world's biggest volcanoes, Mauna Loa and Kilauea, are on the volcanic island of Hawaii. Here, fire fountains erupting from Mauna Loa have created black cinder cones made of ash and bombs (p. 16).

Volcano goddess
Some Hawaiians believe that the goddess Pele makes mountains, melts rocks, and builds new islands. The fiery goddess is said to live in the crater Halema'uma'u, at the summit of Kilauea.

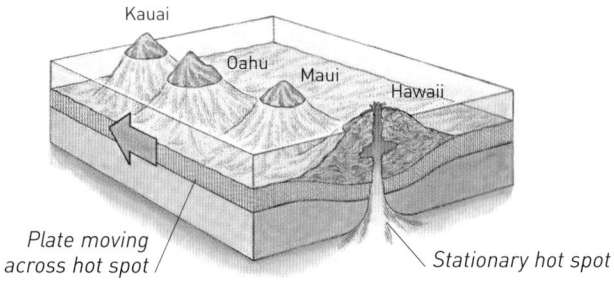

A string of islands
The Pacific Plate is moving over the stationary Hawaiian hot spot, under the south end of the island. In addition to Mauna Loa and Kilauea, a third volcano, Loihi, is growing below the sea to the south. The north end of Hawaii is made up of older, extinct volcanoes.

Pele's hair

The hot, fluid lava of a Hawaiian fire fountain may be blown into fine, glassy strands. These are known as Pele's hair.

Moving hot spot

This volcano is Piton de la Fournaise on the island of Réunion in the Indian Ocean (p. 11). The island is the tip of a huge volcano that rises 4 miles (7 km) above the ocean floor. The hot spot has moved 2,500 miles (4,000 km) in the last 30 million years.

Lava tube

The skin of a pahoehoe flow (p. 19) may crust over into a roof thick enough to walk on. Only a yard or so below, hot lava continues to run in a tunnel or "tube." Lava dripping off the underside of the roof creates strange formations called lava stalagmites and stalactites.

Lava stalagmite made of drips in a pahoehoe tube

Lava has solidified around this tree, leaving a tree mould

Road buried by lava during eruption of Kilauea

Up in flames

Lava in tubes remains hot and fluid, so it can travel many miles, engulfing land and villages on the way.

Ocean floor

New ocean floor is constantly being made by volcanic eruptions beneath the waters. Spreading ridges form where two plates pull apart, creating a rift (crack) in the ocean floor. Here, the lava erupts gently, forming rounded shapes known as pillow lava. This new rock fills in the widening rift as the plates pull farther apart. In this way, the oceans grow just a little wider, half an inch or so, a year. In places, the rifts are bubbling with hot springs, known as black smokers, that are home to a variety of strange life-forms.

Rift through Iceland
The Skaftar rift (above) is part of a 17-mile- (27-km-) long rift that opened in 1783. It erupted more than 3 miles^3 (13 km^3) of lava over eight months. More than 10,000 Icelanders died in the famine that followed.

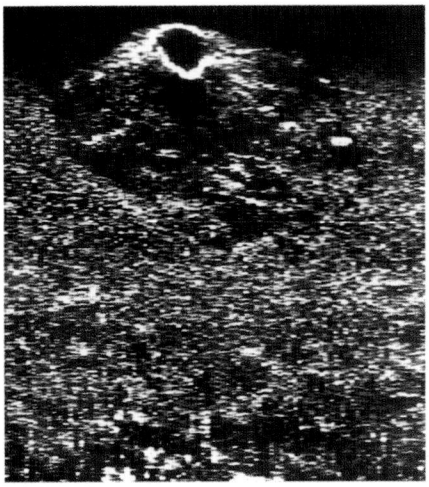

Undersea volcano
This marine volcano lies 13,000 ft (4,000 m) below the Pacific Ocean and measures 6 miles (10 km) across.

Icelandic eruptions give a glimpse of how spreading ridges make new oceanic plate. The eruptions tend to be from long cracks, rather than central craters.

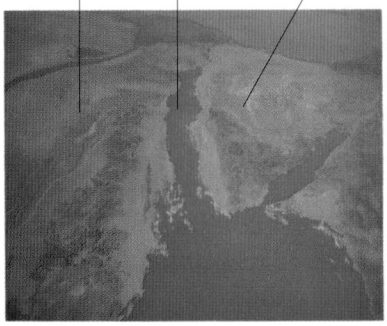

Red Sea
A spreading ridge runs through the Red Sea. For the last 20 million years it has been making a new ocean floor, as Arabia moves away from Africa.

Submersible *Alvin*, taking photos of ridges

Deep-sea shrimp
This new species of shrimp was found at the Galápagos rift in the Pacific Ocean in 1979.

Black smokers

These strange chimneylike structures are found along spreading ridges on the ocean floor. The black, acidic water that gushes from these hot springs is rich in valuable minerals produced by the new ocean plate that is formed at the ridges.

Sulfur-eating tube worms from the Galápagos rift

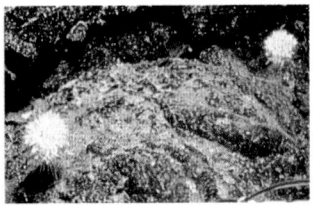

Sea urchins
The animals that live around black smokers include clams and mussels up to 1 ft (30 cm) long. These urchins were seen on the Galápagos rift.

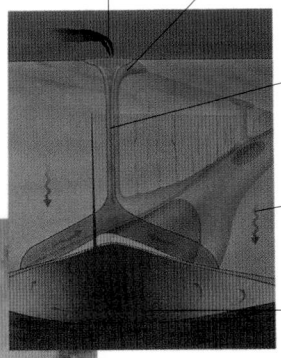

Model of black smoker

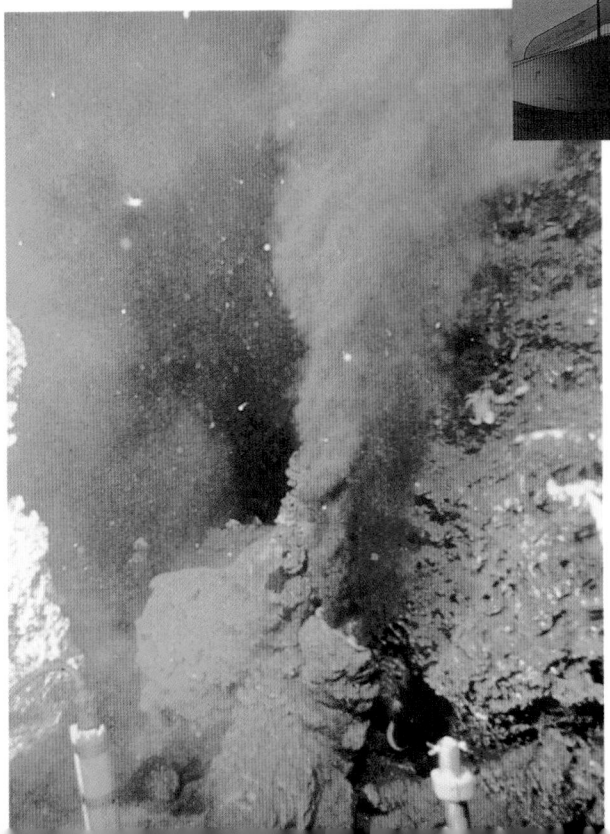

Chimney pipes
When the rising minerals meet the chilled ocean water, they cool and harden to form the chimney pipes that surround the black smokers. These grow steadily, collapsing only when they get too tall.

Rounded, pillow-shaped underwater lava

Manganese nodules
The ocean floor is carpeted with black lumps that are rich in manganese and other metals.

Lava feeder channels
Two ancient lava feeder channels can be seen in the rock above.

Gabbro, a coarsely crystalline rock from an old seafloor magma reservoir in Cyprus

Mount Vesuvius

Pliny the Younger
This scholar watched the eruption from across the Bay of Naples.

Perhaps the most famous eruption of all time was that of Mount Vesuvius, near Naples, Italy. When the long-dormant volcano erupted in 79 CE, the residents of the Roman towns of Pompeii and Herculaneum were caught unawares. Hot ash and stones rained down on Pompeii for hours until it was buried many feet deep. Those trying to flee were overwhelmed by a sudden blast of ash and gas (a pyroclastic surge, p. 16). The buried towns were virtually forgotten until excavations began in the 18th century. These digs have since unearthed priceless treasures.

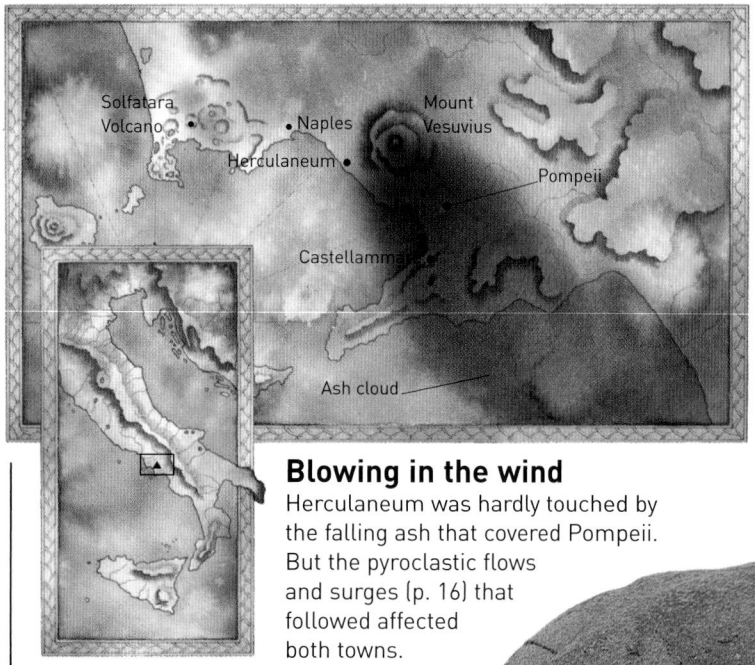

Blowing in the wind
Herculaneum was hardly touched by the falling ash that covered Pompeii. But the pyroclastic flows and surges (p. 16) that followed affected both towns.

Beware of dog
This floor mosaic from a Pompeii entrance hall was designed to warn off intruders.

Burned to a crisp
This carbonized loaf of bread was one of several found in the brick oven of a bakery. The baker's stamp can still be seen, nearly 2,000 years after the day the bread was baked.

Modern Italian bread

Flour mill made of lava, a tough rock also used to pave streets

Portrait of a lady, detail of a floor mosaic found at Pompeii

Bowl of preserved eggs

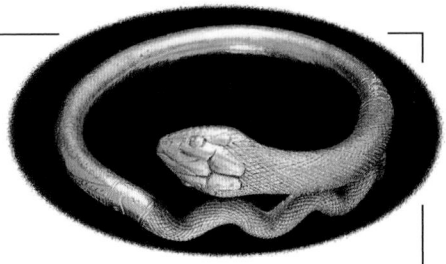

Snake charm

Fine gold and silver jewelry, some set with emeralds, was found in the buried town. This hollow bracelet in the shape of a coiled snake is made of thick gold.

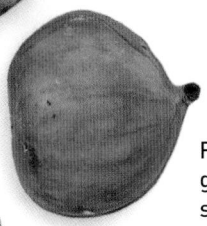

Fresh figs, still grown on the slopes of Vesuvius

Bowl of carbonized figs

Fresh walnuts

Charcoal

Objects that contain carbon, like wood or food, usually burn when heated. But when there is not enough oxygen for them to burn in the normal way, they turn to charcoal instead. This process, called carbonization, left many foods perfectly preserved in the ash.

Bowl of carbonized walnuts

Pompeii destroyed

The large theater (the semicircular building) and the gladiator's gymnasium (in front) can be seen in this artist's impression of the destruction of Pompeii.

Death of Pliny the Elder

In a letter, Pliny the Younger wrote of his uncle and an official fleeing with "pillows tied upon their heads with napkins; and this was their whole defense against the storm of stones that fell around them... my uncle... instantly fell down dead; suffocated... by some gross and noxious vapor... his body... looking more like a man asleep than dead."

Caught in the act of dying

More than 2,000 people died in Pompeii during the eruption. As the fleeing Pompeiians fell, the rain of ash and pumice set around their bodies like wet cement. Over time, the soft body parts decayed and the ash and pumice turned to rock. The shapes of the bodies were left as hollows in the rock with only the hard bones remaining. In 1860, the Italian king appointed Giuseppe Fiorelli as director of the excavations. Fiorelli invented a method for removing the skeletons from the hollows and filling the space with wet plaster of Paris. After the plaster hardened, a true representation of the bodies could be dug out of the rock. Many of these startling casts show people grimacing or huddling together in terror.

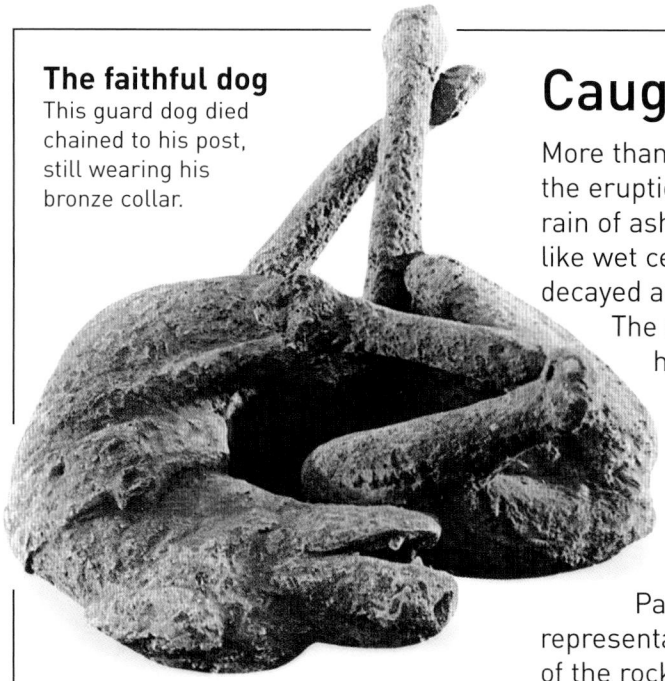

The faithful dog
This guard dog died chained to his post, still wearing his bronze collar.

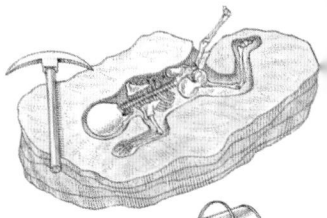

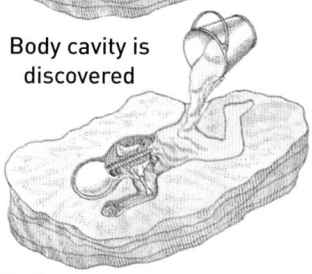

Body cavity is discovered

Cavity is filled with wet plaster of Paris

Last day of Pompeii
This fanciful painting of the destruction of Pompeii by 19th-century German artist Karl Bruillov shows houses catching fire.

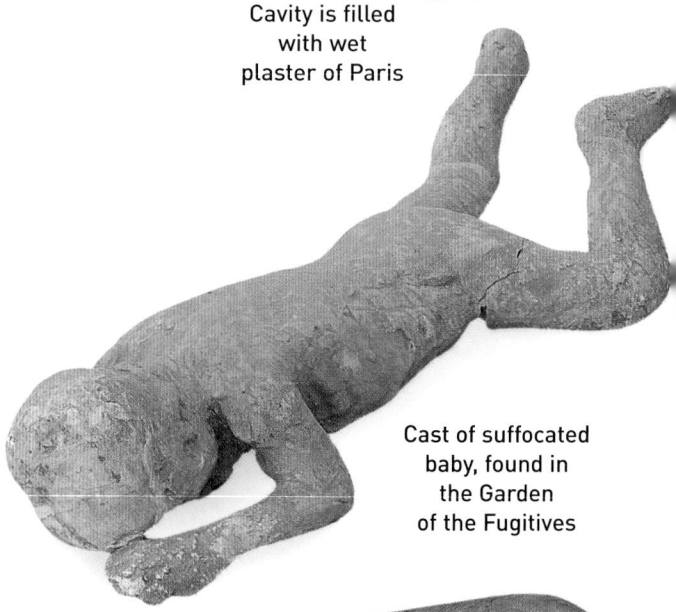

Cast of suffocated baby, found in the Garden of the Fugitives

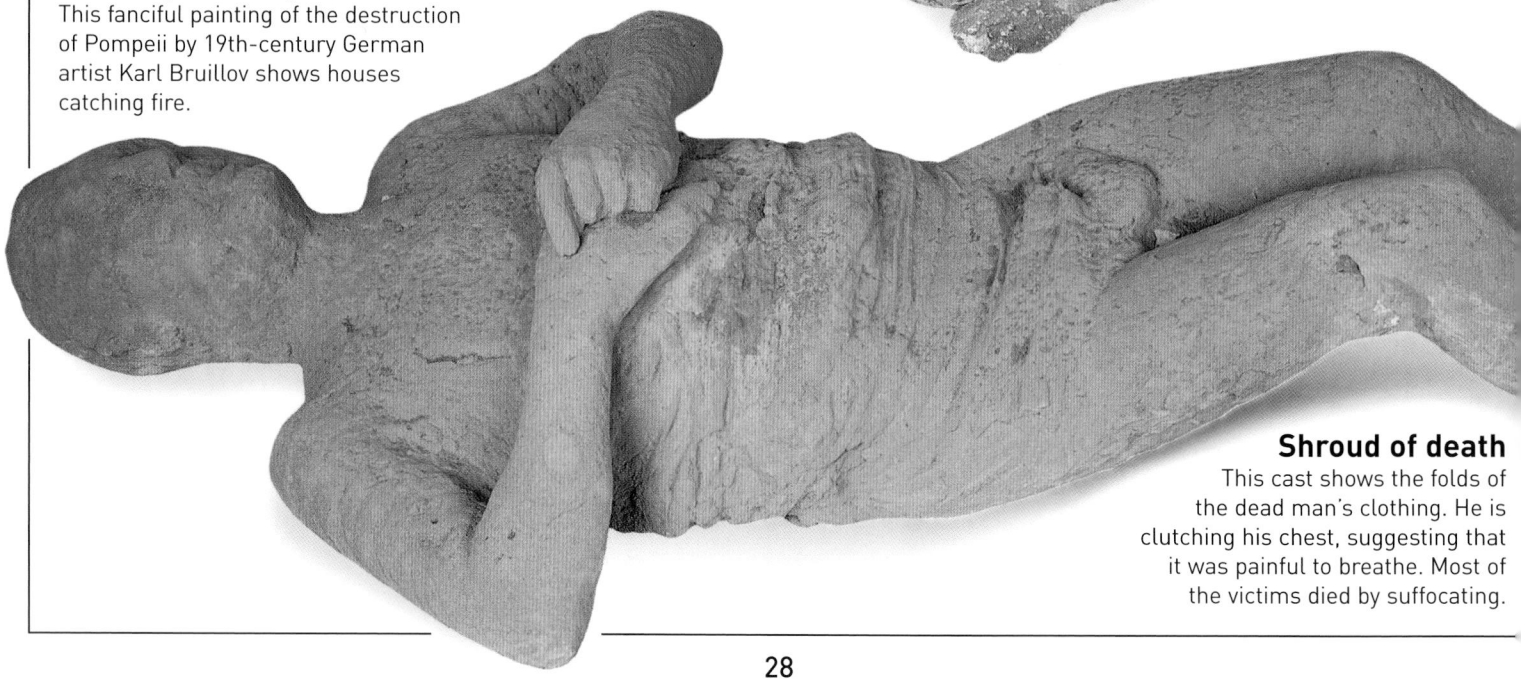

Shroud of death
This cast shows the folds of the dead man's clothing. He is clutching his chest, suggesting that it was painful to breathe. Most of the victims died by suffocating.

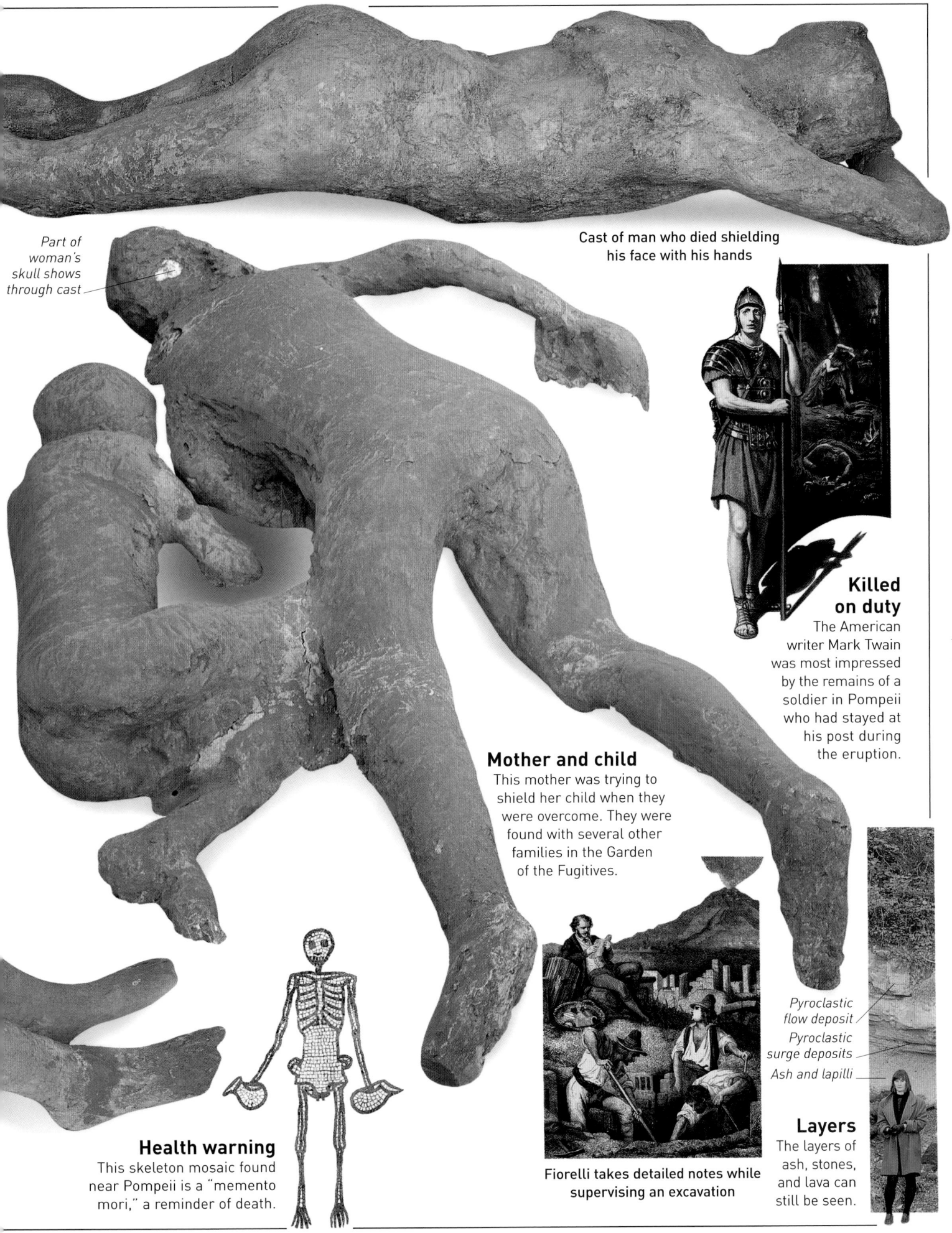

Cast of man who died shielding his face with his hands

Killed on duty
The American writer Mark Twain was most impressed by the remains of a soldier in Pompeii who had stayed at his post during the eruption.

Mother and child
This mother was trying to shield her child when they were overcome. They were found with several other families in the Garden of the Fugitives.

Health warning
This skeleton mosaic found near Pompeii is a "memento mori," a reminder of death.

Fiorelli takes detailed notes while supervising an excavation

Layers
The layers of ash, stones, and lava can still be seen.

Herculaneum

When Vesuvius erupted in 79 CE, the ash cloud that engulfed Pompeii missed Herculaneum (p. 26). Less than 1 in (3 cm) of debris had fallen on the town when it was blasted by a great surge of hot ash and gas. Early excavations uncovered very few bodies, which was puzzling. But in the 1980s, several hundred skeletons were found huddled together beneath huge brick arches that once stood on the shoreline.

Neptune and Amphitrite
This mosaic of two Roman gods was unearthed at a merchant's house in Herculaneum.

Walking in the ruins
The excavations of the Roman town have created a deep hole that is surrounded by the modern city of Herculaneum (p. 60). This street is laid with lava paving stones.

Roman skeletons
Unlike the bones in Pompeii, the skeletons from Herculaneum have no surrounding body shape. This is because they lay in waterlogged ground and the wet ash packed tightly around the bones.

A tomb of hot rock
Herculaneum was hit by six pyroclastic surges (pp. 16–17) followed by thick flows of hot ash, pumice, and rock. These flows buried the town in 65 ft (20 m) of volcanic debris.

1631 eruption

Textbook eruption
This 1767 engraving (above), which probably shows the 1760 eruption, was published in an 18th-century textbook.

Hamilton's view
Lord Hamilton (p. 21), included this view of the 1779 eruption in his book *The Campi Phlegraei*. The artist is Pietro Fabris (p. 39).

The most visited volcano

The Romans who lived in the shadow of Vesuvius were scarcely aware that it was a volcano. The mountain had erupted 800 years earlier, but it had been calm since. The biggest recent eruption, in 1631, produced pyroclastic surges and flows. In the 18th century, travelers flocked to Naples to visit the angry mountain. Even today tourists climb to the summit and pay to look into the steaming crater.

German etching of 1885 eruption showing fires started by lava flows

On the tourist map
This cartoon shows English tourists at Vesuvius in 1890. A guidebook of 1883 advises sightseers to wear their worst clothes because boots could be ruined by the sharp lava and dresses stained by the sulfur.

Photograph of tourists watching the 1933 eruption

Souvenir of Vesuvius
Centuries ago, souvenirs from Naples included Roman artifacts stolen from the excavations. These days security is tighter, and boxes of lava and ash are more common souvenirs.

St. Pierre

One of the worst volcanic disasters of the 20th century happened on the Caribbean island of Martinique. On May 8, 1902, Mount Pelée—the volcano that towered over the city of St. Pierre—erupted just before 8 a.m. The mountain sent a cloud of glowing gas down upon the port and all its inhabitants were engulfed. Within minutes, St. Pierre was charred beyond recognition. A few sailors survived on their ships, but all but two of the city's 29,000 residents were killed.

Statue
The heat pitted the surface of this statue. The other side (which faced the volcano) shows more damage.

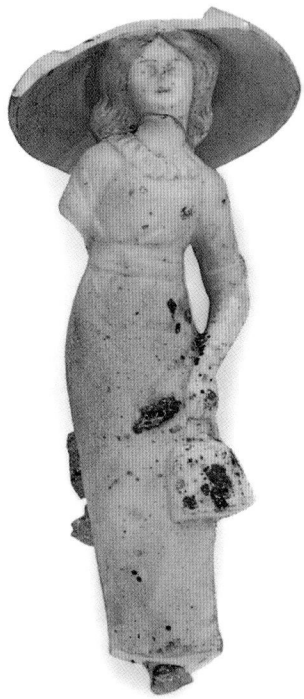

Broken statuette

Stopped clock
This pocket watch was melted to a standstill at 8:15 a.m.

Alfred Lacroix
French volcanologist Alfred Lacroix arrived in St. Pierre on June 23. In his report on Mount Pelée, he described strange "glowing clouds." Today these are known as pyroclastic flows or surges (p. 16).

Melted medicine bottle

Melted wine bottle

Melted metal fork
(rust occurred after eruption)

Melted glass
Discovered in the 1950s, these partly melted objects give a glimpse of everyday life in the small French colony at the beginning of the 20th century. Some objects are either so melted or so unfamiliar that it is hard to guess what they are.

Remains of mousetrap

Top of charred human femur (thighbone)

Ruined city
The walls of some buildings were all that was left standing in St. Pierre. Many died in the cathedral, where mass had just begun.

Protecting angel?
This angel figurine, made of metal is just about recognizable.

Heap of glass melted beyond recognition

Charred mug

Squashed candlestick

Petrified
Some objects containing carbon were scorched or burned completely. Others were carbonized (pp. 26–27).

Carbonized coffee beans

Melted metal
Many metal objects melted in the heat. These iron nails fused together, while the metal spoon lost part of its bowl. The candlestick was probably squashed by a falling building. Copper telephone wires in the town were not melted, so the temperature of the cloud must have been less than 1,981°F (1,083°C), the melting point of copper.

Heap of fused iron nails

Eternal figure
The wooden cross was burned off this crucifix, leaving just the figure of Jesus.

Fused coins

Melted metal spoon

Out of the frying pan
One of the two survivors in St. Pierre was Auguste Ciparis, a condemned prisoner. He survived because his cell had thick walls and a tiny window. He was later pardoned and became part of a circus act.

Affecting the world's weather

Early Earth
About 4 billion years ago, planet Earth had no atmosphere and its surface was covered with erupting volcanoes. All the water in the oceans and many of the gases that make up the atmosphere have been produced by volcanic eruptions.

A big ashy volcanic eruption has a dramatic effect on the weather. Dark days, severe winds, and heavy rain may plague the local area for months. If the gas and dust are thrown high into the atmosphere, they can spread round the world, affecting the climate of the whole planet. The volcanic material filters out some sunlight, reducing temperatures down below. In the longer term, volcanic particles may cause global cooling, mass extinctions, or even ice ages.

Little Ice Age
Two major eruptions in Iceland and Japan in 1783 led to several icy winters in Europe and America.

Dinosaurs
It is likely that the dinosaurs died out due to climate change caused by a major asteroid impact and huge volcanic eruptions that occurred around 65 million years ago.

Volcanic sunset
Eruptions can cause unusually red sunsets. This sunset was caused by dust from the 1980 eruption of Mount St Helens (pp. 14–15).

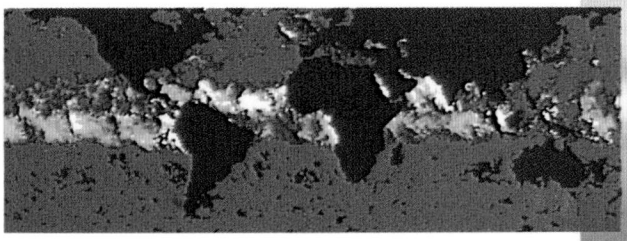

Floating around the globe

The June 1991 eruptions of Mount Pinatubo in the Philippines (right and p. 17) spewed ash and gas into the stratosphere. Satellite images (above) showed that by July 25 the particles had spread around the world.

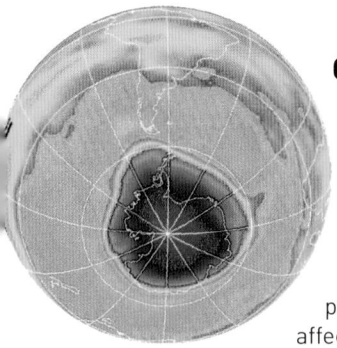

Ozone hole

This false-colored satellite image shows the hole in the ozone layer over the Antarctic. Sulfur particles thrown up by Pinatubo may cause further damage to this protective layer. This could affect world temperatures.

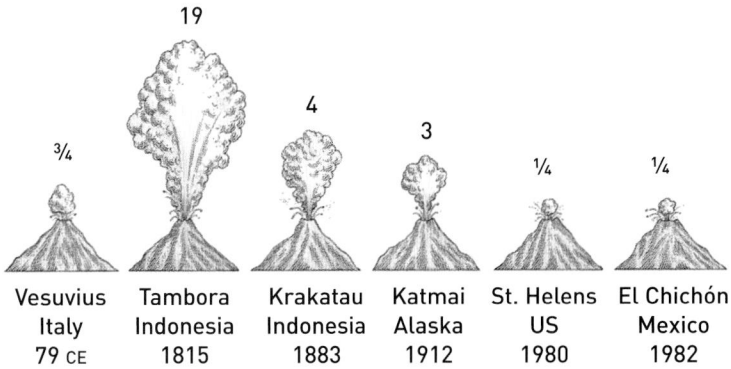

Comparing the size of eruptions

The amount of ash a volcano spews out is a good measure of the size of the eruption. This diagram compares the amounts of ash produced in six major eruptions. The units are cubic miles.

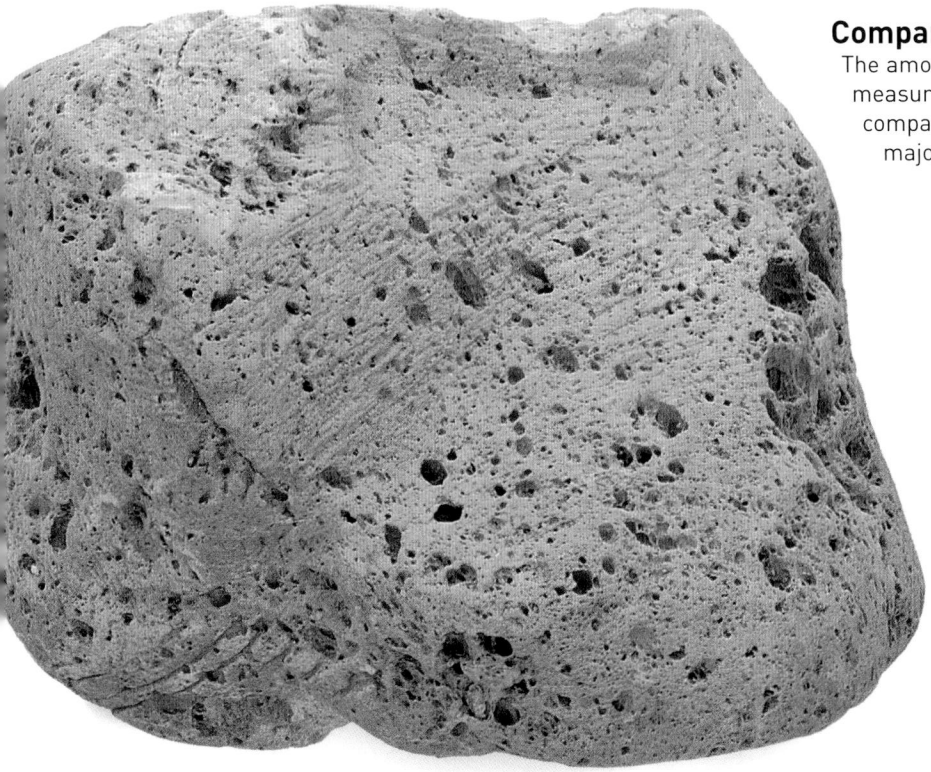

Krakatau

In 1883, the Indonesian island of Krakatau was blown to pieces in a massive eruption (p. 57). The explosion was heard 2,500 miles (4,000 km) away in Australia. Floating islands of pumice drifted across the Indian Ocean for months afterward. This piece was washed up on a beach in Madagascar, 4,500 miles (7,000 km) away.

An artist's impression of the 1883 eruption of Krakatau, Indonesia

In hot water

In volcanic areas, heat from the rocks also heats the water in the ground. During long dormant (inactive) periods, the hot water may shoot to the surface in steam vents, geysers, hot springs, and pools of bubbling mud. These hydrothermal (hot water) features can be put to good use. Steam can be used to generate electricity, and hot groundwater can help to heat homes and greenhouses.

Vulcan, god of fire
The ancient Romans believed Solfatara volcano in Italy was one of the workshops of the blacksmith god Vulcan—hence our word "volcano."

Measuring the Earth's heat
An instrument called a thermocouple (p. 43) is being used to measure the heat of a steam vent, or fumarole, in the Solfatara crater. Temperatures here can reach 284°F (140°C). Changes in the heat and gas can give clues to future volcanic eruptions.

Healing powers
The fumaroles in Solfatara give off acid gases as well as steam. The steam that emerges from the caves is meant to have miraculous healing powers. Since Roman times, visitors have taken steam baths to treat arthritis and breathing problems.

Crystals of sulfur
The sulfur in volcanic gas cools and forms crystals. These huge, yellow crystals are from Sicily, where sulfur has been mined for centuries. Sulfur has many uses, particularly in manufacturing. It is added to rubber to make it more durable in a process called vulcanization—named after the Roman god Vulcan.

Bubbling mud

Some fumaroles bubble up through a mud bath of their own making. The acid sulfur gases eat into the rock they pass through, creating a pot of soft mud. The mud in this pot at Solfatara is 140°F (60°C). Some mud pots are much hotter, while others are cool enough for people to relax and bathe in.

Smelly gas

Sulfur crystals can be clearly seen around this fumarole vent. Close to the vent, the hot, smelly gases are invisible. Like the steam from a kettle, they show up only when the water vapor begins to condense (turn into water) an inch or so away.

Roman baths

The ancient Romans built huge public baths with hot running water. Baths fed by natural hot springs became medical centers where sick people came to bathe in the mineral-rich water.

Crust of tiny sulfur crystals from fumarole in Java, Indonesia

Souvenir plate showing Old Faithful Geyser, US (p. 7)

Hot water power

About 40 percent of Iceland's electricity comes from hydrothermal power plants. Countries such as Japan and the US are also developing hydrothermal power programs.

Sleeping beauties

Church built on eroded remains of old volcano, Le Puy, France

Volcanoes sometimes sleep (lie dormant) for years, or even centuries, between eruptions. In this dormant period, volcanic gases may seep gently from the magma beneath the volcano. As these gases rise through the rocks of the volcano mountain, they react chemically with minerals already in the rocks to create new minerals. These are often brightly colored with large crystals. At Earth's surface, the gases fume gently off into the atmosphere.

Radiating zeolite crystals from the Faëroe Islands

Born in the lava
Zeolite crystals grow in old gas bubbles in lava. They are found in a variety of colors and forms.

Agates
These beautiful banded stones form in cavities in cooled or cooling volcanic rocks. Each band is formed at a different time period.

Outer layers of this agate are oldest

Adventurers descend into the crater of Hekla, Iceland, in 1868

Crater lake
Craters often fill with rainwater. This crater lake, on the Shirane volcano in Japan, is very acidic due to gas seeping up from the magma chamber. In an eruption, the acidic water mixed with hot rock and debris could cause a deadly mud flow (pp. 56–57).

Brightly colored rocks seen by Lord Hamilton at Solfatara (pp. 36–37) and illustrated by Pietro Fabris

Olivine from St. John's Island in the Red Sea

Precious stones

Chemicals in the hot volcanic fluids cool slowly inside gas bubbles or in other cavities in the volcanic rock. This process often produces large crystals that can be cut and polished into gemstones. Hard stones, like diamonds, are the most prized because they last forever.

Cut diamond

Uncut diamond in volcanic rock from the mantle, from Kimberley in South Africa

Cut peridot

Red Sea gem

Gem-quality olivine is a deep green color. The gem is known as peridot.

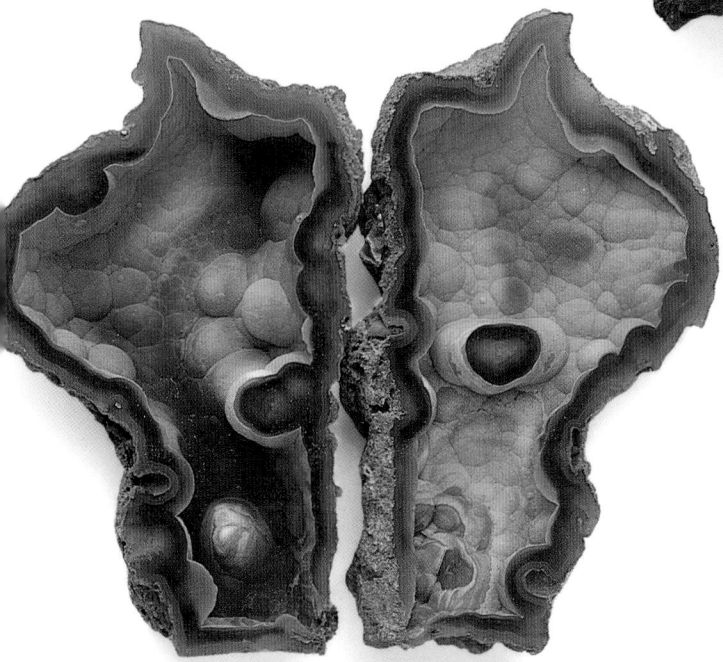

Agate-lined geode (cavity) from Brazil

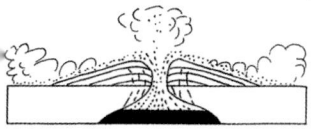

Birth of a caldera

During a large ashy eruption, the empty magma chamber may not be able to support the volcano's slopes. These collapse inward, leaving a huge dip called a caldera.

Santorini

This Greek island is the rim of a caldera formed by a huge volcanic eruption c. 1620 BCE. The massive explosion may have led to the collapse of the Minoan civilization on the neighboring island of Crete.

Sleeping volcano

Mount Rainier is one of a chain of volcanoes in the Cascade Range, US. There are no records, but the volcano probably erupted several times in the 1800s. These events can be dated from tree rings, which show stunted growth after an eruption.

Life returns

Volcanic eruptions can have a dramatic effect on the landscape. Volcanic ash is full of nutrients that enrich the soil, but too much can be catastrophic for farmers. Thick, sticky lava covering the land can take months to cool. Decades may pass before plant life returns to the landscape. Only when a rich soil covers the ground is it lush and fertile again. This process can take generations.

1944 lava flow, Mount Vesuvius

Raw lava

Dense, interlocking crystal structure

Putting down roots

Ferns, mosses, and lichens are some of the first plants to grow after an eruption. Here, a fern takes root in a ropy pahoehoe lava flow less than a year old on the slopes of Kilauea, Hawaii (pp. 22–23).

A few lichens find a home on the lava

Grasses, often the first flowering plants to grow

Beginnings of topsoil

Lichen cling to exposed parts of rock

Lichen covers the lava, providing a soft surface for other plants

Rock breaks down to soil, and grass and moss take root

Two species of moss grow in thin soil

Gathering moss

The rate at which plants grow back after an eruption depends on the type of erupted material. Plants are slowest in taking root on lava flows; they grow more quickly in ashy, pyroclastic material (p. 14). These lava pieces are all from the 1944 aa flow on the west slope of Mount Vesuvius in Italy. Some 47 years later, lichen covers a lot of the flow, and moss, grasses, and weedy flowering plants are taking root.

New cone is still bare ash

Monte Somma, part of caldera (p. 39) left by huge, prehistoric eruption

Pine forests cover lower slopes

Mount Vesuvius steaming after mild eruption of 1855

Birth of an island
In November 1963, an undersea eruption off southwest Iceland gave birth to a new island, Surtsey (p. 20).

Washed ashore
Seeds blown over or washed up on the beach of Surtsey soon took root in nearby ashfields (above).

Through the grapevine
The land around Vesuvius has been fertilized by ash from regular eruptions over the last 20 centuries. Grapes grown in the lush soil are used to make wine.

Peacock butterfly lives on nectar of flowering plants

Lacrima Christi
Mount Vesuvius is shown on the label of this wine grown on the volcano's slopes. Without the nutrients from the volcanic ash, the vines would not grow so thickly and the wine would taste less sweet.

Eventually, the soil is thick enough to support larger plants

Flower of Lydia
This brilliantly colored shrub, a kind of broom, is one of the first plants to grow on the lava at Vesuvius.

Roman amphorae
The stacks of amphorae for storing wine and olive oil found at Pompeii (pp. 26–31) show how fertile the soil was in Roman times.

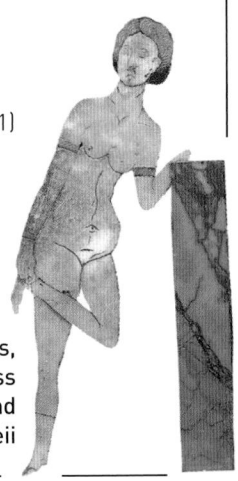

Mosaic of Venus, Roman goddess of fertility, found in Pompeii

Studying volcanoes

Volcanologists—scientists who watch, record, and interpret volcanoes—spend years monitoring volcanoes to try and predict when and how they will next erupt. Most of their work involves analyzing data, but fieldwork on the slopes of active volcanoes is vital. This involves taking lava and gas samples and measuring changes in landforms and temperature—usually while wearing protective clothing.

Katia Krafft
French volcanologists Maurice and Katia Krafft (left) spent their lives documenting volcanoes. Sadly, the husband and wife team were killed during the eruption of Mount Unzen in Japan in 1991.

Spaced-out suit
This protective suit has a metal coating that reflects the heat of the volcano and leaves the person inside cool. Heat-proof boots are worn to walk across the red-hot lava.

Volcano notebook
The volcanologist makes notes and sketches of everything that takes place during an eruption. The significance of some things may only become clear later.

Hot rod

This metal rod is ideal for collecting red-hot lava. The volcanologist dips the end into the lava flow, then twists it around, hooking up a blob of lava.

Tape measure

A tape measure is handy for checking cracks in the ground that may widen by a minuscule amount each day.

A closer look

Binoculars allow people to observe a volcano from a safe distance.

Gloves made from the heat-resistant mineral asbestos

Too hot to handle

Volcanologists wear asbestos gloves to pick up red-hot lava. Hard hats protect against volcanic bombs (p. 18).

Pathfinder

This mining transit (left) is a useful tool for mapping the ground of a volcano. It has a compass and a level (to check verticals and horizontals). Small and light, it can be clipped onto the volcanologist's belt.

Mapping the moving Earth

A precise level is used to detect the small changes in ground level that occur before an eruption.

Folding, portable tripod

Taking the volcano's temperature

Katia Krafft takes the temperature of a lava flow on Piton de la Fournaise volcano, Réunion (pp. 22–23). She is using an electric thermometer called a thermocouple. The reading was 2,000°F (1,100°C).

Other planets

The many space missions over the past few decades have brought back photographs of volcanic activity on other planets. Like Earth, the Moon, Venus, and Mars have surfaces that have been partly shaped by volcanic activity. The volcanoes on the Moon and Mars have been extinct for many millions of years. Scientists suspect that Venus's volcanoes may still be active. But of all the other planets in our solar system, only Io, one of Jupiter's 16 moons, shows volcanoes that are still erupting.

Housekeeping
The hero of Antoine de Saint-Exupéry's children's story *The Little Prince* lives on a planet with two active volcanoes. Before setting out on a journey, he cleans them out to be sure they won't erupt and make trouble while he's away.

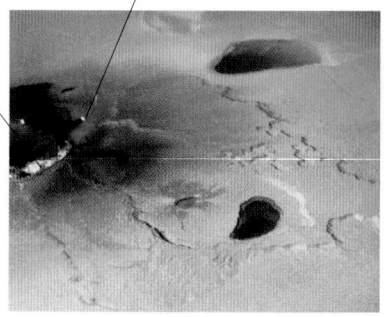

Surface of Io
This colored infrared image shows a volcanic region on the surface of Io. The image shows molten rock and a 37-mile- (60-km-) long lava flow, produced by a volcanic eruption.

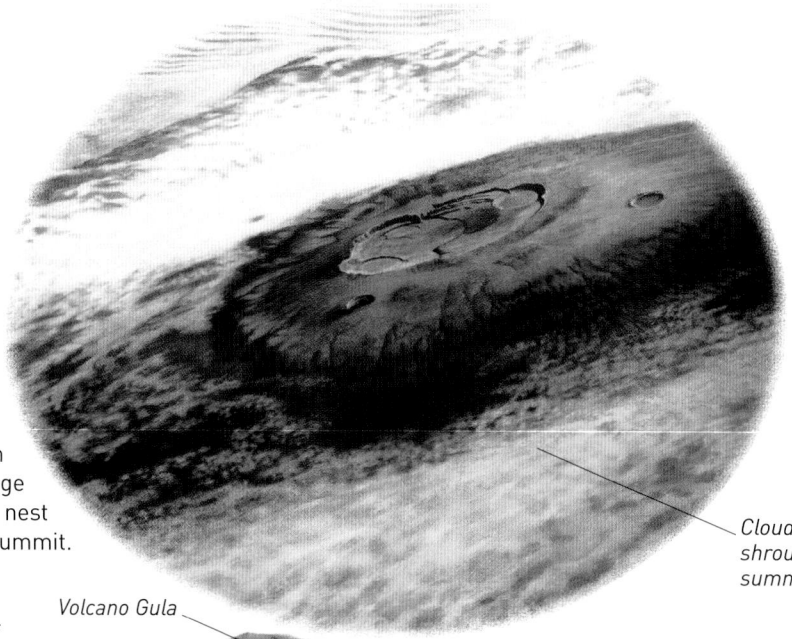

Olympus Mons
The extinct volcano Olympus Mons is 375 miles (600 km) across and rises 16 miles (25 km) above the surrounding plain. It is the largest volcano to be found in the universe so far. Huge calderas (p. 39) nest inside one other at its summit.

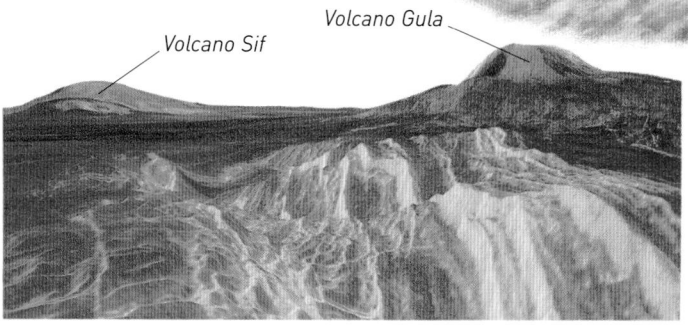

Beneath the clouds
The spacecraft *Magellan* used imaging radar to penetrate the dense atmosphere of Venus. The images revealed huge volcanoes lurking beneath the clouds. They were named after women, including goddesses from mythology.

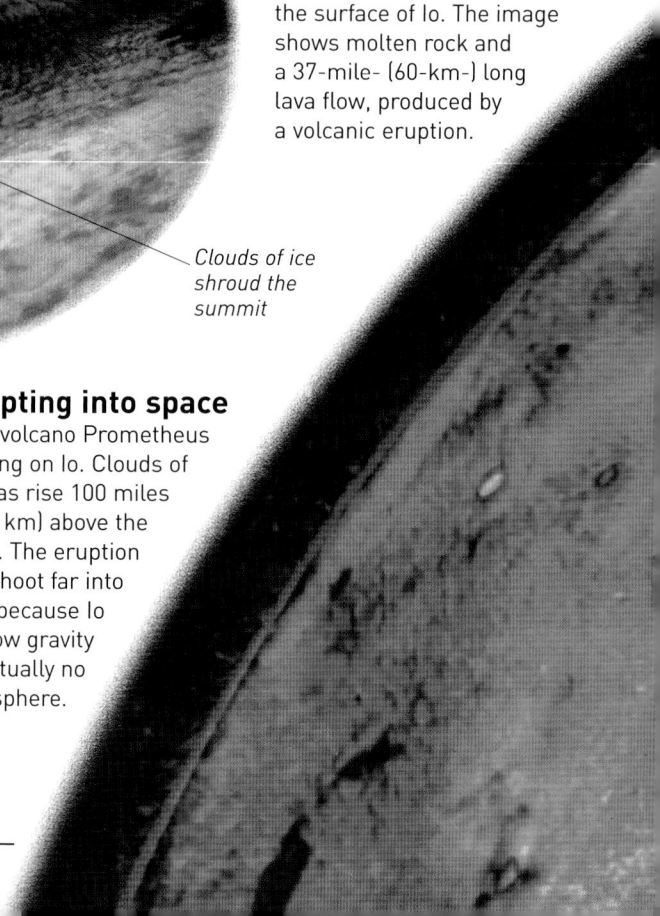

Erupting into space
Here, the volcano Prometheus is erupting on Io. Clouds of gas rise 100 miles (160 km) above the surface. The eruption clouds shoot far into space because Io has very low gravity and virtually no atmosphere.

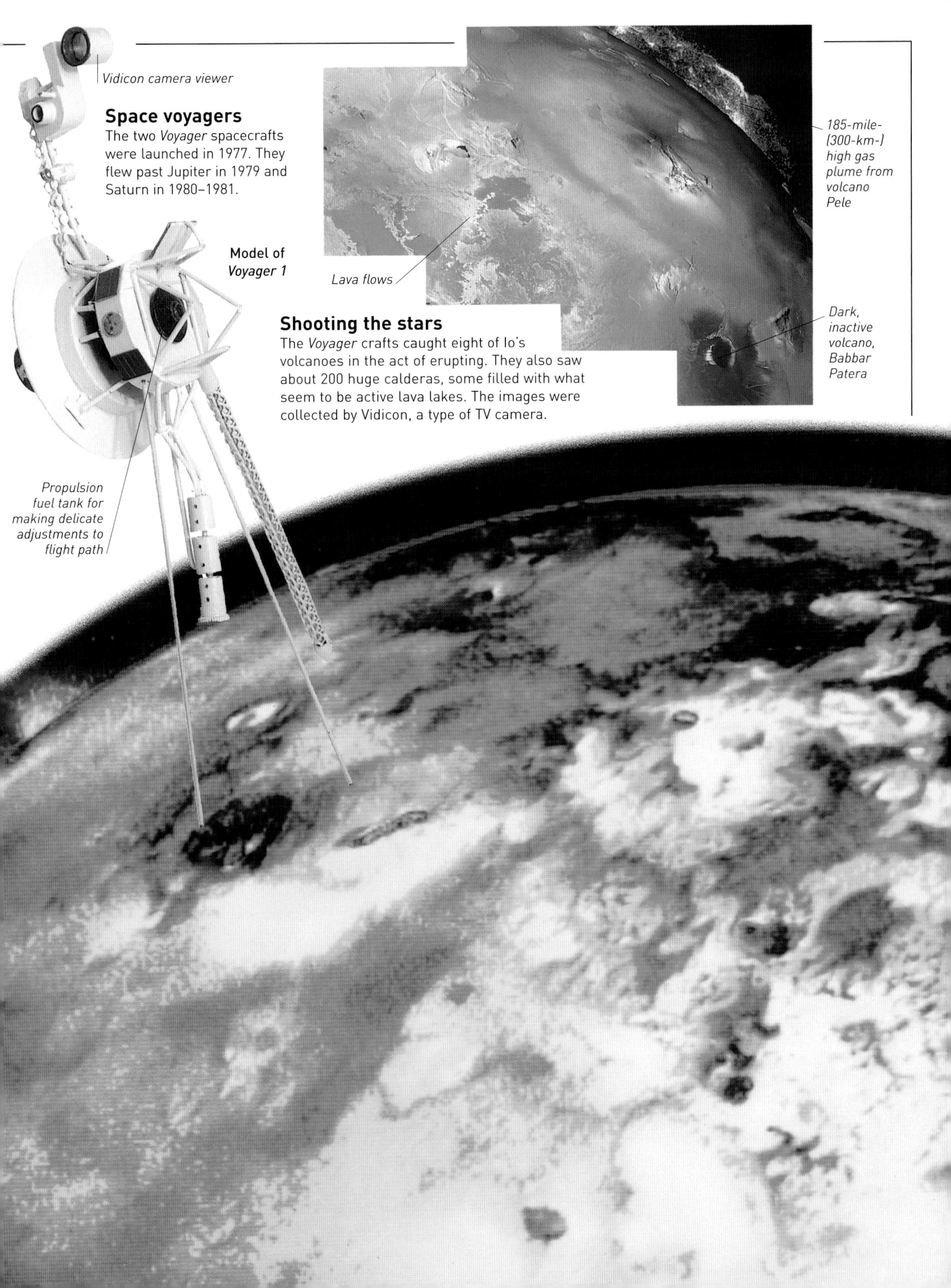

Space voyagers

The two *Voyager* spacecrafts were launched in 1977. They flew past Jupiter in 1979 and Saturn in 1980–1981.

Shooting the stars

The *Voyager* crafts caught eight of Io's volcanoes in the act of erupting. They also saw about 200 huge calderas, some filled with what seem to be active lava lakes. The images were collected by Vidicon, a type of TV camera.

1906 cartoon, captioned "I hope I never have one of those splitting headaches again."

When the earth moves

Being in a large earthquake is a terrifying experience. When the shaking starts there is no knowing how long it will go on or how severe it will be. The longest tremor ever recorded, the Alaskan earthquake of March 23, 1964, lasted four minutes. But most quakes last less than a minute. In those brief moments, homes, stores, and even entire cities are destroyed. Afterward, great cracks may appear in the ground. Aftershocks, which follow a big tremor, can continue for months.

Shaken to the foundations
Almost 75 years old, these wood buildings in San Francisco slipped off their foundations during the 1989 earthquake (p. 7).

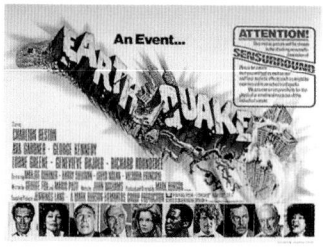

Disaster movie
This earthquake movie was shown in "Sensurround"—low frequency sounds meant to simulate earthquake shaking.

Panic sets in
People leave buildings and rush into the streets in panic as an earthquake shakes the city of Valparaiso, Chile, in 1906.

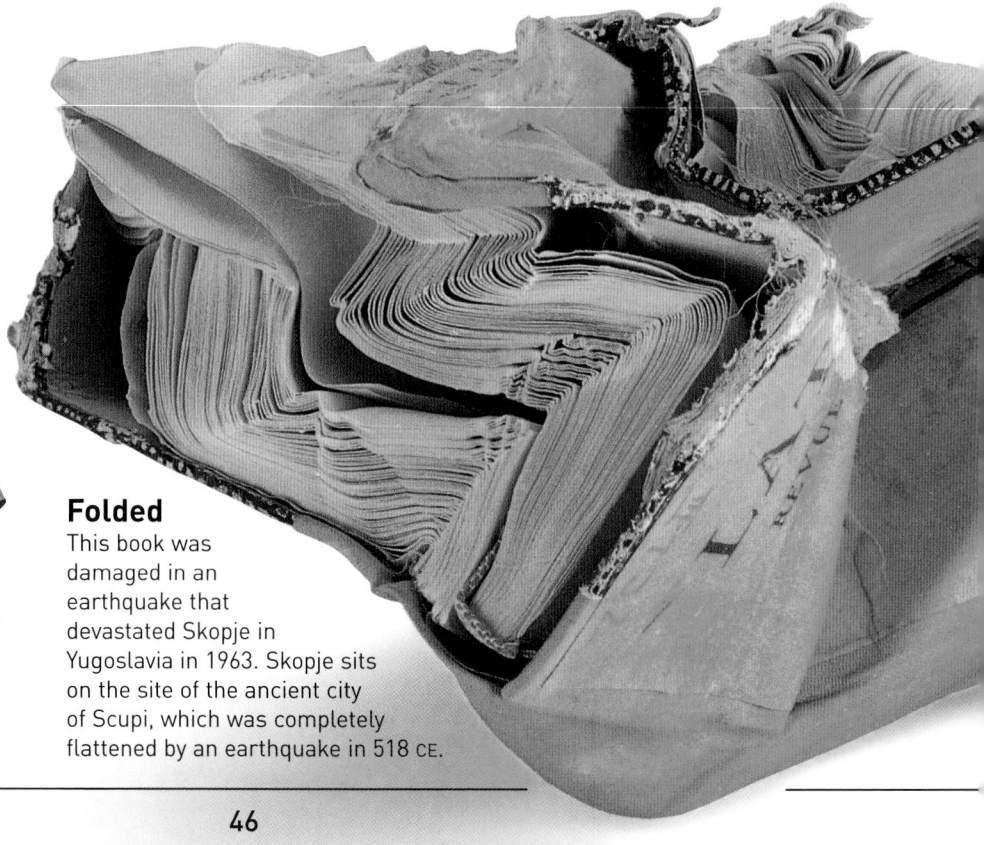

Folded
This book was damaged in an earthquake that devastated Skopje in Yugoslavia in 1963. Skopje sits on the site of the ancient city of Scupi, which was completely flattened by an earthquake in 518 CE.

Temple of Jupiter

Rocking the temple

The Roman town of Pompeii was hit by a large earthquake in 62 CE. A marble carving from a house in the town shows the damaged Temple of Jupiter.

When the earth breaks

Solid rocks can fracture when the earth shakes. This road cracked during an earthquake measuring 6.9 on the Richter scale (pp. 48–49).

Cracking ground

Volcanic tremors are caused by moving magma. Here, rising magma has cracked the ground before an eruption of Piton de la Fournaise volcano, Réunion.

Shaken up

The Roman philosopher Seneca wrote about the earthquake that damaged Pompeii in 62 CE. He was particularly interested in the psychological effects of the ground shaking and the fear it caused.

Solid as a rock?

This piece of limestone has a natural polish caused by earthquake stresses and strains. The flat surface was almost melted by the heat generated as the rock broke.

Voltaire

The French writer Voltaire (1694–1778) wrote about the huge Lisbon earthquake of 1755 in his novel *Candide*. The novel made fun of religious figures who said that God was punishing the residents for their immoral ways.

Shaking, fire, and flood

The 1755 quake destroyed three-quarters of Lisbon's buildings. Huge tsunamis (pp. 56–57) destroyed the harbor, and more than 10,000 people were killed.

Intensity and magnitude

How do you measure the size of an earthquake? News reports usually give the quake a magnitude on the Richter scale. The Richter magnitude is useful because it can be worked out from a recording—called a seismogram—of the earthquake waves (pp. 52–55). These waves can be recorded from anywhere on the planet. The intensity of the shaking and how it affects buildings and people cannot be recorded by a machine. It is compiled by inspecting damage and measured on a scale such as the Modified Mercalli Intensity Scale.

Giuseppe Mercalli (1850–1914)

Intensity

The Italian volcanologist Giuseppe Mercalli created his intensity scale in 1902. He used 12 grades with Roman numerals.

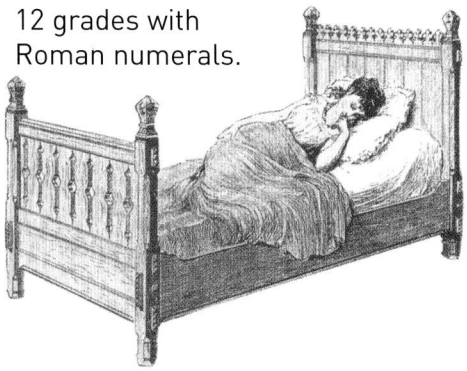

I The shaking is not felt by people, but instruments record it.

II People at rest notice the shaking (above), especially if they are on upper floors of buildings. Lightly suspended objects may swing.

III People indoors feel a vibration like the passing of a light truck. Hanging objects start to swing (above).

IV Vibration like a heavy truck passing. Dishes rattle and standing cars rock.

V Felt outdoors. Liquid in glasses slops out (above). Small objects fall.

VI Felt by all. Many are frightened and rush outdoors. People walk unsteadily; dishes and windows break (above).

Magnitude

In the 1930s, Charles Richter wanted to compare the sizes of local earthquakes. First, he calculated the distance between himself and the earthquake. He then used this distance, together with the wiggly tracings of the ground movement (pp. 52–55) to come up with the magnitude.

American seismologist Charles F. Richter (1900–1985)

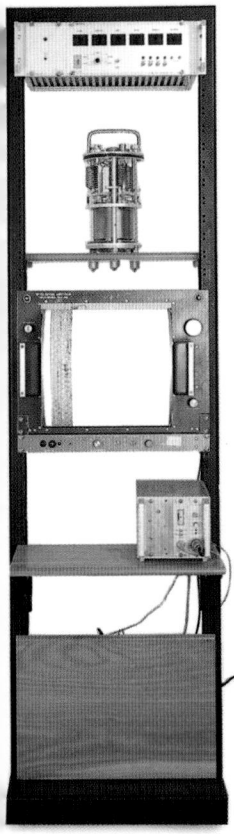

Recording shakes
Richter took the smallest earthquake he could record at the time and called it magnitude zero. The highest Richter magnitudes recorded are about 9.

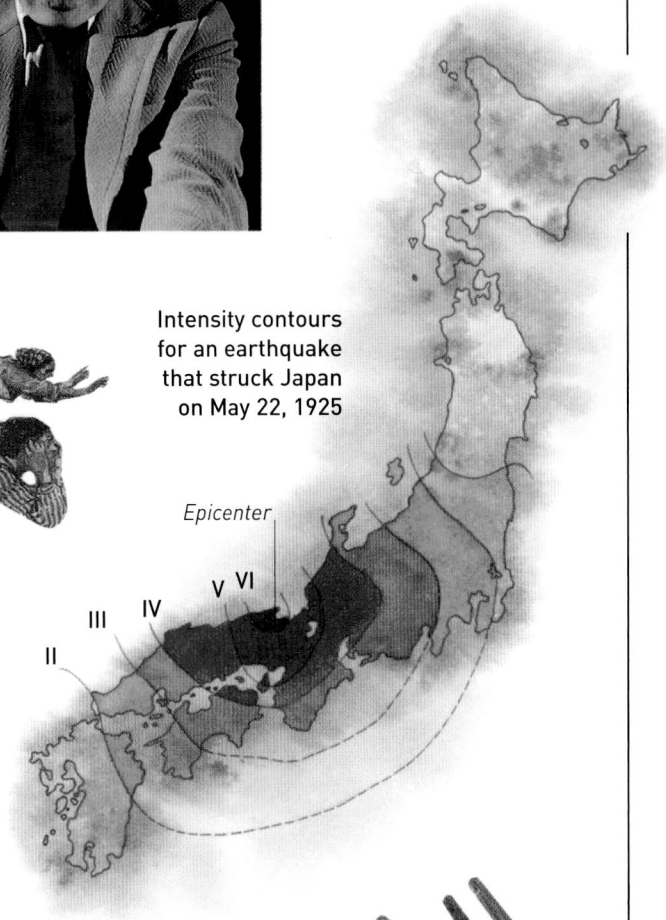

Intensity contours for an earthquake that struck Japan on May 22, 1925

VII Difficult to stand (above). Plaster and loose bricks crack and fall. Waves on ponds. Bells ring.

VIII Steering of cars affected. Damage to walls, some of which fall. Falling chimneys, steeples (above). Cracks in wet ground.

IX Panic. Animals run in confusion. Frame buildings, if not bolted down, shift off their foundations (above). Mud and water bubble out of ground.

X Masonry and frame buildings destroyed (above). Some well-built wooden buildings destroyed. Large landslides. Water thrown out of rivers.

XI Railroad lines greatly distorted. Underground pipelines out of service. Highways useless. Large cracks in ground. Large rockfalls.

XII Practically all built structures destroyed or useless (above). Ground much altered with cracks. River courses moved. Waterfalls appear.

Shock waves

Earthquake waves travel fast—about 15,500 mph (25,000 kph) in rock. In the seconds after the rock fracture that causes the earthquake, shock waves travel out in all directions. Usually they are most devastating near the epicenter—the place on the Earth's surface nearest to where the rocks have fractured. But sometimes the waves are slowed down by soft sands and muds. This can cause severe shaking even far from the epicenter.

Seismogram

This is a recording of a 5.1 magnitude quake. The primary (P) waves arrive first, followed by slower secondary (S) waves. The time lag between the P and S waves—17 seconds—is used to calculate the distance from the epicenter.

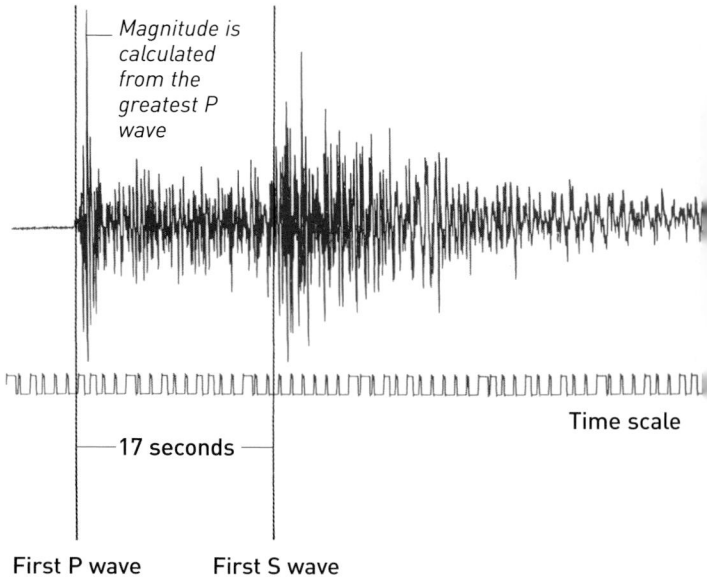

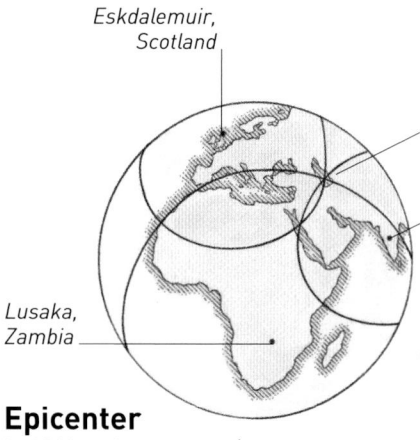

Epicenter

In 1989, seismologists (people who study earthquakes) in Scotland, Africa, and India calculated how far away a quake had struck and drew a circle across the globe based on their results. The circles met in the Caspian Sea, the epicenter of the quake.

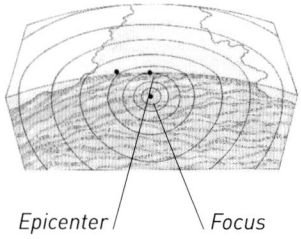

Deep focus

An earthquake's focus—the area where the rocks have fractured—is usually many miles inside the Earth.

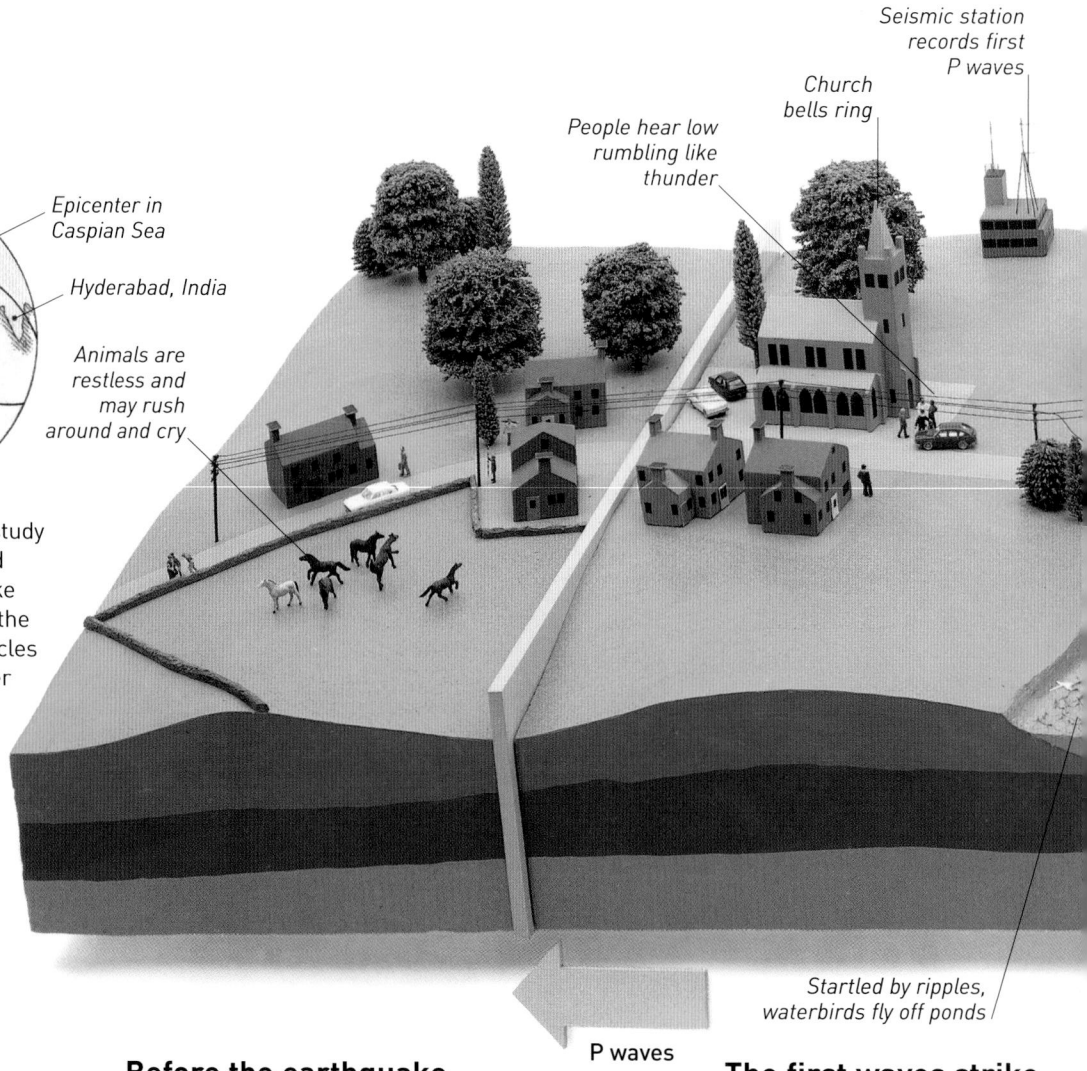

Before the earthquake

Animals often sense something is wrong in the minutes before an earthquake strikes.

The first waves strike

The first P waves to arrive may be so small that they are heard but not felt.

Devastated in a minute

In 1843, the town of Pointe-à-Pitre on the island of Guadeloupe was hit by an earthquake of magnitude 8. The shaking lasted for about a minute—long enough to reduce most of the buildings to ruins. A fire that followed destroyed what was left of the town.

Woman sits by the ruins of her house in Lice, Turkey

Living through an earthquake

This model shows the waves from a large earthquake. The fast P waves (yellow) are about to strike the area on the far left. S waves (blue) follow, causing considerable damage. The slowest, surface waves (red), arrive seconds later, causing the total collapse of buildings already weakened by the S waves.

Ground cracks open

Trees and bushes shake and rustle

Cracks appear in buildings

Vehicles cannot follow straight lines

Sand and water bubble out of ground for hours after shaking stops

Fires start in ruins

Trees are uprooted

Landslide

People panic, have trouble standing up

Many buildings in ruins

S waves

Surface waves

Secondary waves strike

The S waves following the P waves are shaking buildings until they crack or collapse.

Surface waves

Some quakes produce surface waves that cause serious damage far from the epicenter.

Measuring earthquakes

The first instrument for recording earthquakes was built by the Chinese scientist Zhang Heng in the second century CE. The device, known as a seismoscope, could record earthquakes too slight to be noticed otherwise. In 1856, a more sophisticated device was invented by the Italian Luigi Palmieri. His seismograph was designed to measure the overall size of the earthquake shaking (pp. 48–49).

Early seismologist
The Chinese were keeping lists of earthquakes as early as 780 BCE. But it was not until 132 CE that the Chinese astronomer Zhang Heng (78–139) invented the first seismoscope. The bronze device measured about 6½ ft (2 m) across.

Inner workings of Zhang Heng's seismoscope

Suspension mechanism pulls on dragon's mouth

Pendulum

Seismoscope
During a tremor, the vessel moves more than the heavy pendulum hanging inside. This triggers one or more of the dragons to open their jaws and release a bronze ball into the mouths of the toads below.

Ball held in dragon's mouth

The toad that is farthest from the epicenter catches the falling ball. This indicates which direction the quake came from

Ring my bell

This reconstruction of a seismoscope (left) was built by Italian naturalist and clockmaker Ascanio Filomarino in 1795. When the ground shook, the pendulum stayed still. But the rest of the apparatus shook, making bells ring and a clock tick.

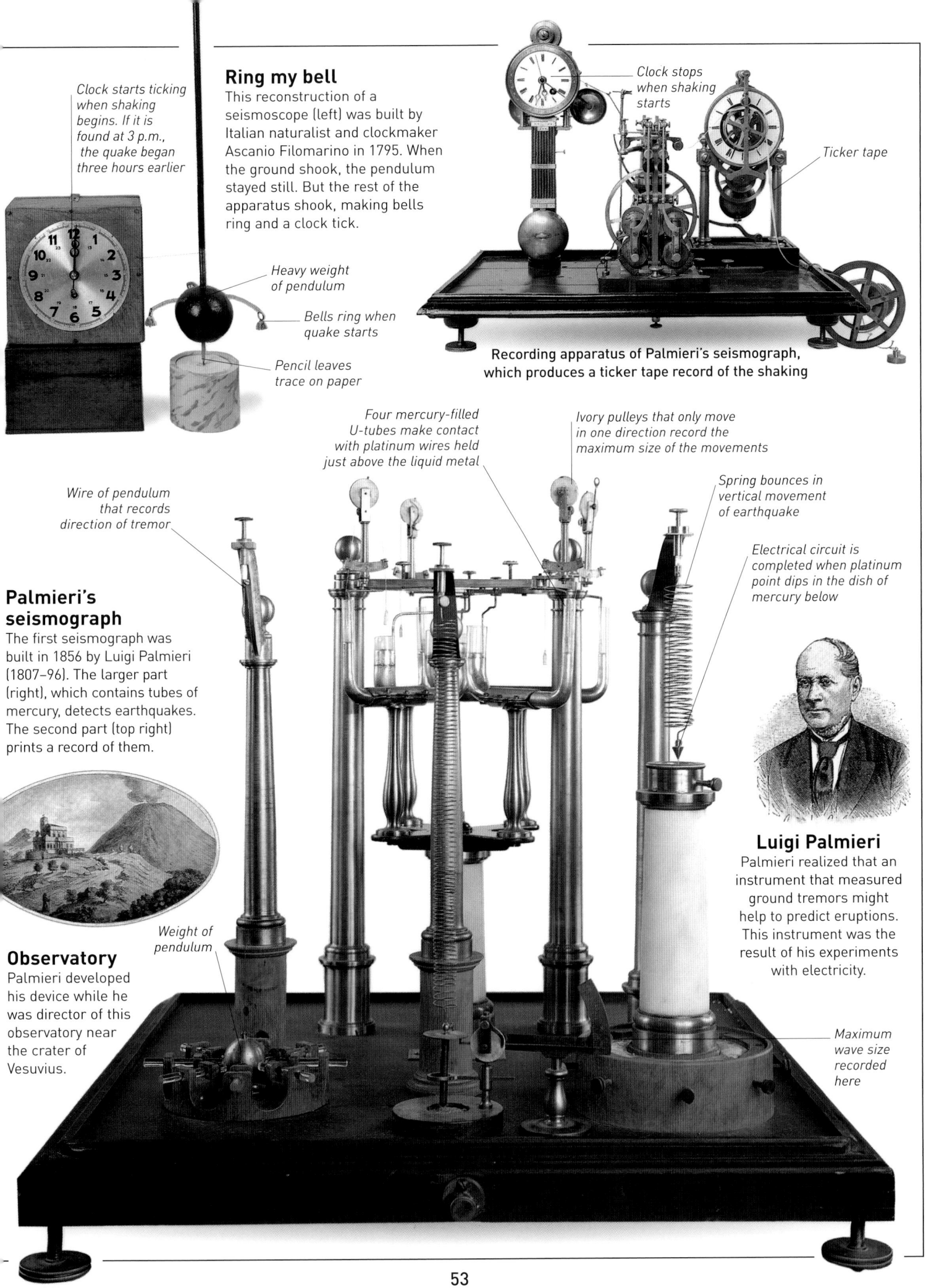

Recording apparatus of Palmieri's seismograph, which produces a ticker tape record of the shaking

Palmieri's seismograph

The first seismograph was built in 1856 by Luigi Palmieri (1807–96). The larger part (right), which contains tubes of mercury, detects earthquakes. The second part (top right) prints a record of them.

Observatory

Palmieri developed his device while he was director of this observatory near the crater of Vesuvius.

Luigi Palmieri

Palmieri realized that an instrument that measured ground tremors might help to predict eruptions. This instrument was the result of his experiments with electricity.

Tokyo, 1923
This photo shows the city of Tokyo after the huge quake of 1923. At least 200,000 died in the fire storm that followed.

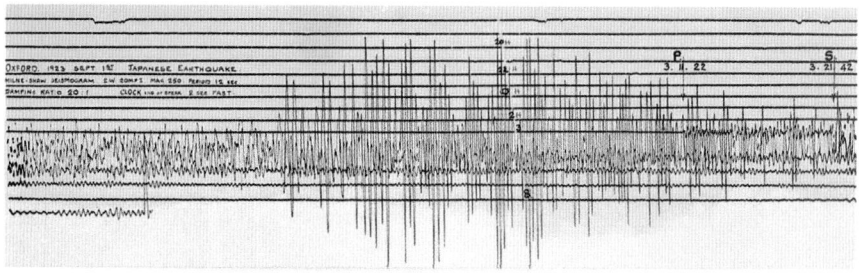

Seismogram of 1923 Tokyo earthquake, recorded by the Gray-Milne seismograph in Oxford, England

John Milne
An English geologist, John Milne (1850–1913) invented his own seismograph while he was teaching geology in Tokyo.

Seismometers

Seismometers capture earthquake movement. They work on the principle that an earthquake shakes a heavy pendulum less than the surrounding ground.

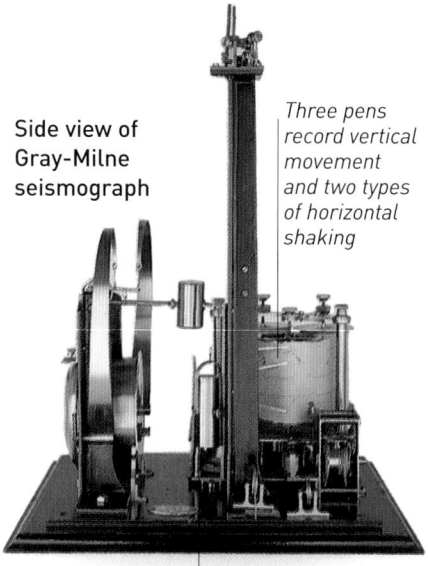

Side view of Gray-Milne seismograph

Three pens record vertical movement and two types of horizontal shaking

Pendulum to record horizontal shaking

Clock shows the moment the quake starts

Ground motion
This seismograph, designed by Thomas Gray and John Milne, had three pendulums and three pens to record the three types of ground motion—vertical, east-west horizontal, and north-south horizontal.

A modern observatory

At the Vesuvius Observatory, great reels of paper record the ground movement measured by a series of seismometers. Their data is beamed into the recording center by radio or along telephone lines. Modern seismographs record on magnetic tape, which allows for much better analysis.

Portable

Networks of portable seismometers are used to monitor the aftershocks of big quakes and ground tremors during volcanic eruptions.

Moonquakes

American astronauts left seismometers on the Moon to record moonquakes. Many moonquakes are caused by meteorites hitting the surface.

Paper drum winds very slowly between earthquakes. When shaking starts, gears change and the drum starts feeding the paper through much faster

Case hides suspended pendulum

Handle for winding up weight that turns drum

Damping system, which makes sure that each shock wave is only recorded once

Suspended weight drives paper drum (mechanical clocks driven in same way)

Smoked paper seismogram

Arm from which pendulums are suspended

Smoking up

Early seismographs, many still in use, scratch their traces on smoked paper. This prevents the problem of ink running out—a disaster during tremors.

Heavy duty

This is a restored version of the seismograph invented in 1908 by German scientist Emil Wiechert (1861–1928). Its 440 lb (200 kg) mass measures the two horizontal movements of ground shaking. It worked with a smaller instrument that measured vertical motion.

Mud, fire, and floods

The events that follow an earthquake or volcanic eruption can be even more dangerous than the disaster itself. Heavy rain mixed with volcanic ash can create devastating mud flows. In mountains, both quakes and eruptions may trigger landslides and avalanches; by or beneath the sea, they can both cause giant water waves known as tsunamis.

Swept away
The ashy eruptions of Mount Pinatubo in the Philippines (p.17) were accompanied by mud flows that swept away roads, bridges, and several villages.

Overview of Armero mud flow, 1985

Buried in mud
In 1985, the Ruiz volcano in Colombia, South America, spewed clouds of ash and pumice onto snow and ice at the mountain's summit. The melted snow and ash formed a heavy mud flow that traveled at speeds of up to 22 mph (35 kph). In the city of Armero, 37 miles (60 km) away, some 22,000 people were buried alive by the waves of mud, rock, and debris that set around them like wet concrete.

Lorry trapped in mud, Armero

Pozzuoli

The town of Pozzuoli near Naples, Italy, has been shaken by many small earthquakes. Part of the town was abandoned after shaking damage in 1983. The town has risen several yards since then, so the harbor had to be rebuilt lower down.

Dwarfing Fuji

Tsunamis are caused by both volcanic eruptions and earthquakes. The volcano Fujiyama in Japan is shown in this picture of a tsunami by Katsushika Hokusai (1760–1849).

Tsunami

In 2011, an earthquake with 9.0 magnitude hit Oshika Peninsula in Japan, causing a tsunami. More than 18,000 people were killed. The tsunami also caused a system failure in the nuclear power plant Fukushima Daiichi. As a result, tons of radioactive water leaked into the Pacific Ocean.

Krakatau, west of Java

Tsunamis as high as 100 ft (30 m) crashed into surrounding islands after the eruption of Krakatoa (now called Krakatau, p. 35). More than 36,000 people were killed.

Fire in the ruins

These firefighters are putting out a blaze after the 1989 San Francisco earthquake (p. 7). The fires that follow quakes or eruptions can completely destroy cities. If gas mains are broken or inflammable liquids spilt, the slightest spark causes fire. Shaking often damages water supplies, making a blaze harder to fight.

Avalanche

In 1970, a magnitude 7.7 quake off the coast of Peru caused a disastrous slide of snow and rock. The avalanche fell 13,000 ft (4,000 m) and killed more than 50,000 people in the valley below.

State of emergency

The chaos that follows a big earthquake or volcanic eruption makes rescue difficult and dangerous. Half-collapsed buildings may topple farther at any moment. Hazardous substances could suddenly catch fire or explode. In ash-flow or mud-flow eruptions, no one knows when to expect another surge. Damage to electricity, gas, and water supplies and disruption to communication links make rescue operations even harder to mount.

Perilous rescue
A survivor is lifted by helicopter in Armero, Colombia, in 1985 (p. 56).

Muddy escape
A survivor is rescued from the boiling mud flows that engulfed Armero in 1985. Many survivors had to be treated for burns.

Finding live bodies
A thermal image camera is used to locate people trapped after an earthquake. Survivors are often buried, wounded or unconscious in the rubble of their collapsed homes. The camera uses infrared radiation to detect the heat of a living person.

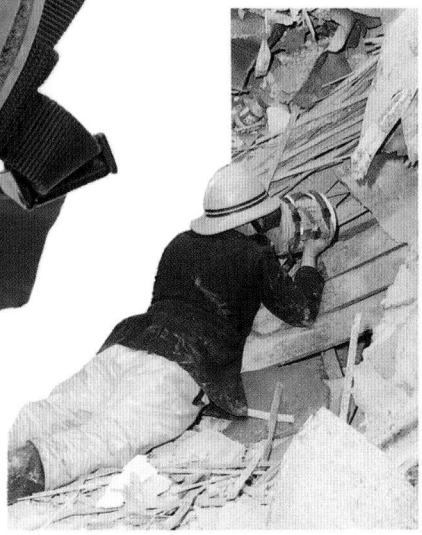

Helping out
The London Fire and Civil Defence Authority sends trained teams to disaster zones like northwest Iran after the massive quake of June 1990.

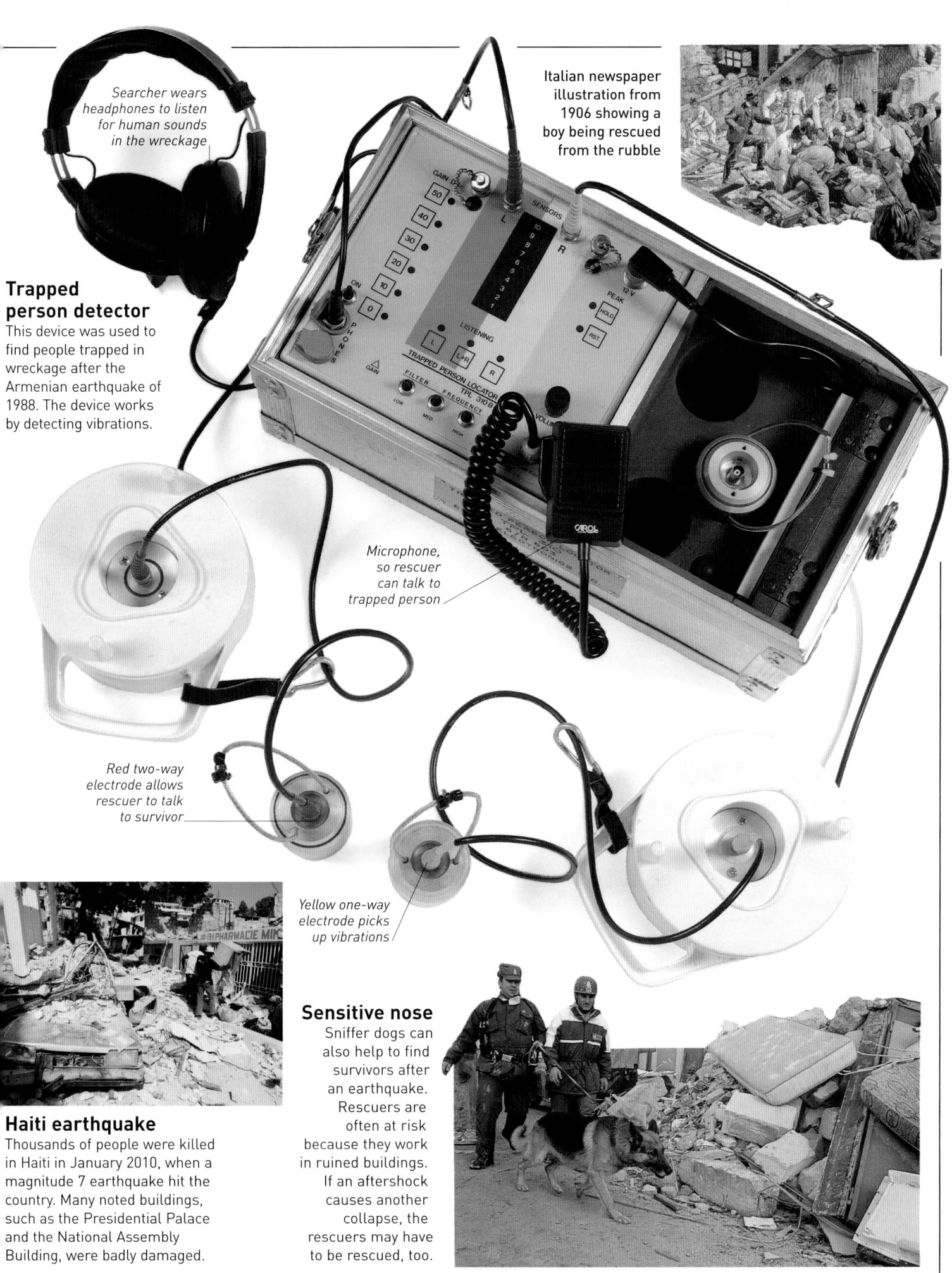

Searcher wears headphones to listen for human sounds in the wreckage

Italian newspaper illustration from 1906 showing a boy being rescued from the rubble

Trapped person detector

This device was used to find people trapped in wreckage after the Armenian earthquake of 1988. The device works by detecting vibrations.

Microphone, so rescuer can talk to trapped person

Red two-way electrode allows rescuer to talk to survivor

Yellow one-way electrode picks up vibrations

Haiti earthquake

Thousands of people were killed in Haiti in January 2010, when a magnitude 7 earthquake hit the country. Many noted buildings, such as the Presidential Palace and the National Assembly Building, were badly damaged.

Sensitive nose

Sniffer dogs can also help to find survivors after an earthquake. Rescuers are often at risk because they work in ruined buildings. If an aftershock causes another collapse, the rescuers may have to be rescued, too.

One step ahead

As the planet's population increases, more people are living in danger zones, along faults or close to active volcanoes. We cannot hope to stop disasters entirely, but we can reduce their number and scale. Learning to live in disaster zones means monitoring volcanoes and fault lines and building cities that can withstand earthquakes. It also means educating people to know what to do in an emergency.

Italian magazines produced for the 1990s, the International Decade for Natural Disaster Reduction

Earthquake-proof cities
Many modern buildings in earthquake-prone cities are designed to withstand shaking. The Transamerica Pyramid in San Francisco looks precarious, but in a major quake the structures at the base will reduce sway by a third.

In the shadow of Vesuvius
Two thousand years after the volcano's greatest eruption (pp. 30–31), modern Herculaneum (above) is a thriving town.

Frank Lloyd Wright
This American architect was a pioneer in the design of earthquake-resistant buildings. His Imperial Hotel in Tokyo survived the 1923 quake almost unscathed.

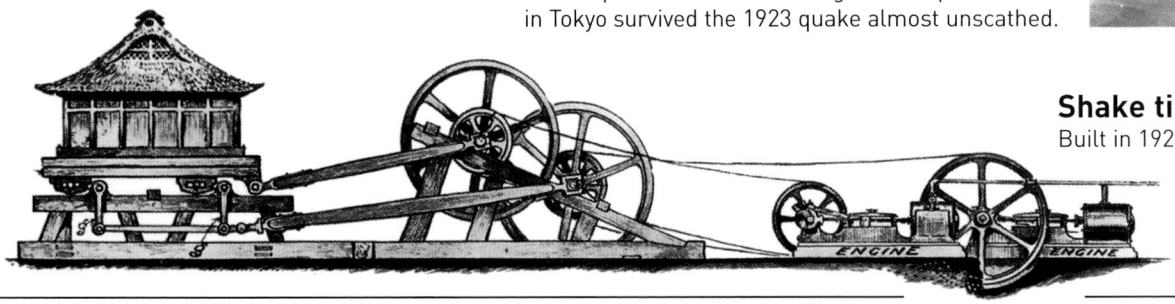

Shake till they drop
Built in 1923, this Japanese shaking table was used to test models of buildings to see how they stood up to severe shaking.

Most measured place

The town of Parkfield in central California lies above the San Andreas fault system. Seismologists (pp. 48–49) have predicted a major earthquake here. A laser measuring system is being used to detect movements along the fault. It can detect ground movement of less than a millimeter over a distance of 3¾ miles (6 km).

Measuring creep

A technician for the US Geological Survey has been measuring creep—slow movement along the fault.

Learning from the past

Earthquakes of the same size tend to happen in the same place at regular intervals. Studying large quakes—in this case, the one that rocked Pompeii in 62 CE (p. 47)—may help scientists to predict the next big tremor.

Falling masonry

In this earthquake drill, rescue workers are treating actors "hit" by falling masonry. Designing buildings without heavy stone ornaments or chimneys might help to reduce the numbers of casualties like these.

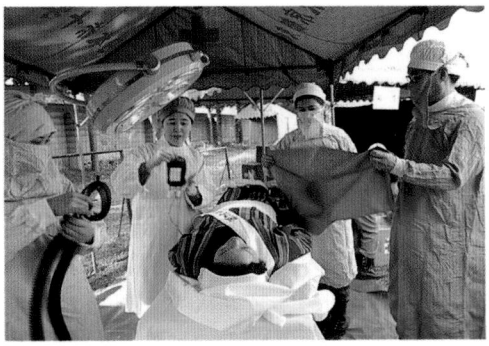

Earthquake rescue practice in Japan

Earthquake drill

In Japan and California, earthquake drills are part of everyday life. Children learn to keep a flashlight and shoes by their beds, so they can get to safety at night. The safest place indoors is under a piece of furniture like a table, or beneath a door frame.

Anger of the gods

As long as people have lived on Earth, they have been curious about natural events like volcanic eruptions and earthquakes. Myths and legends are a way of recording or explaining these strange happenings. For centuries, many societies have explained natural events as the workings of a god or gods. It was thought that angry gods would punish people with a fiery eruption or the horrible shaking of an earthquake. Some societies still believe that certain gods live on the eerie summits of volcanoes, which are often shrouded in fire and cloud.

Christians in Naples, Italy, try to stop the 1906 eruption of Mount Vesuvius (p. 31) with crosses and prayers

Human sacrifice
In Nicaragua, people used to throw young women into the lava lake at Masaya to stop the volcano from erupting.

Popocatépetl
This Aztec illustration shows Popocatépetl in Mexico. When the volcano erupted violently in the 1520s, the Aztecs believed it was because the gods were angry with the Spanish conquerors who had looted their temples.

Lava lake

Responsible frog
Many cultures believed that the ground they stood on was held up by some huge creature. The Mongolians believed this was a gigantic frog. Each time the animal stumbled under his great burden, the ground shook with an earthquake.

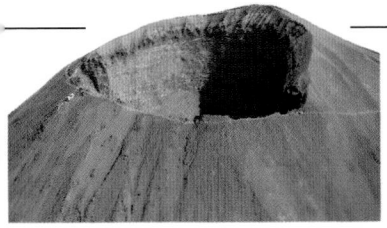

One-eyed giant

From above, the craters on Mount Vesuvius look like giant eyes. They may have inspired the Greek myth of the Cyclops, a tribe of one-eyed giants who helped the fire god Hephaistos (below).

Shaking the seafloor

When the Greek sea god Poseidon was angry he banged the seafloor with his trident (spear). The ancient Greeks believed that this led to earthquakes and tsunamis (pp. 56–57).

Destruction of Sodom and Gomorrah, by an unknown Flemish painter

Sodom and Gomorrah

According to the Bible, God destroyed these cities with flood and fire because the inhabitants were evil.

Bronze figure of Hephaistos, 1st or 2nd century BCE

Master of fire

The ancient Greeks believed the god Hephaistos had his fiery workshops under volcanoes (p. 36). Another god, Prometheus, stole some of the fire from the volcanoes and gave it to humans.

When the gods are away...

A Japanese myth says earthquakes were caused by a giant catfish. Normally the fish was pinned down by a large rock. But when the gods were away, the creature could escape. This print shows the gods flying back after a big quake, carrying a rock.

Home of the gods

Mount Fuji in Japan is thought to be the home of the god Kunitokotache. The sacred spirit of the mountain, Fujiyama, is said to protect the Japanese people.

Did you know?

FASCINATING FACTS

Much of New Zealand's North Island, and all island life, were devastated by the eruption of the Lake Taupo caldera in 180 CE. Luckily, the first human inhabitants did not occupy the island until 1000 CE.

Around 200 black bears were killed in the eruption of Mount St. Helens.

Figures from Mount St. Helens estimate that 11,000 hares, 6,000 deer, 5,200 elk, 1,400 coyotes, 300 bobcats, and 15 mountain lions were killed by the blast.

Pyroclastic flows can travel at up to 300 mph (500 kph) and reach temperatures of 1,500°F (800°C), burning everything in their path.

Where cracks form in the ocean floor, the water heated by magma can reach temperatures of 1,224 °F (662°C).

One of Iceland's greatest attractions used to be the Great Geyser, near Reykjavik, which had a jet 200–260 ft (60–80 m) high. The geyser stopped spouting in 1916.

When Krakatau in Indonesia erupted in 1883, the noise was so loud it burst the eardrums of sailors over 25 miles (40 km) away. Around 36,000 people died, most killed by tsunamis—some 100 ft (30 m) tall—that devastated Java and Sumatra. Villages, ships, and boats were swept inland.

Fires are a major problem after an earthquake. Fractured gas pipes mean fires spread rapidly and burst water mains dry up the hoses. This, together with streets blocked with debris, make the firefighters' work near impossible.

The greatest volcanic eruption in modern times was Tambora, Indonesia, in 1815. It produced 19 miles^3 (80 km^3) of volcanic ash, compared with 0.25 miles^3 (1 km^3) measured at Mount St. Helens. In the past 10,000 years, only four eruptions have been as violent as Tambora.

A tsunami can travel at speeds of up to 375 mph (600 kph).

A steamer swept inland at Krakatau

Animals often act strangely before an earthquake. In 1975, in China, scientists correctly predicted an earthquake when they noticed snakes waking up from hibernation and rats swarming.

A truck flees from the burning clouds of Pinatubo, Philippines, 1991

Pyroclastic flows traveling at over 40 mph (70 kph) were recorded

QUESTIONS AND ANSWERS

Q When is a volcano said to be extinct rather than dormant?

A A volcano is classified as active if it has erupted within the last few hundred years. It is dormant if it has not erupted in the last few hundred years but has erupted during the last several thousand years. If a volcano has not erupted during the last several thousand years, it is said to be extinct.

Q Have people ever tried to stop an advancing lava flow?

A When the volcano on the Icelandic island of Heimaey erupted in 1973, the residents tried to save the harbor on which the island depended from the lava. They did not stop it, but by spraying 6 million tons of seawater at the lava, they slowed it down and slightly altered its course. The lava flow stopped just 450 ft (137 m) from the harbor.

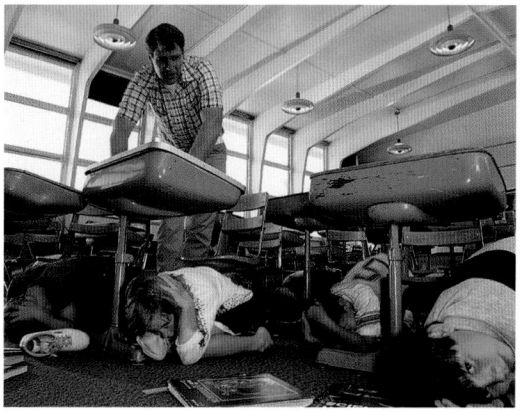

Earthquake drill at a school in the US

Q What should you do if there is an earthquake?

A Shelter in a doorway or under a strong table and protect your head with your arms. When the tremors stop, leave the building, and shelter away from walls, which may collapse.

Q How many active volcanoes are there in the world?

A There are more than 1,500 active volcanoes that rise above sea level. On average, around 20–30 are actually erupting each month. Some of these are volcanoes that erupt continually, like Mauna Loa and Kilauea.

Mauna Loa, Hawaii

Q Could lava just come out of a crack in the earth?

A Yes, in 1943, in Paricutin in Mexico, a farmer found lava pouring from a crack in his field. Within a day there was a cone 30 ft (10 m) high. After a year of eruptions, the lava was 1,500 ft (450 m) tall and had engulfed the nearby town.

A church tower rises from the lava of Paricutin

Paricutin, Mexico, buried by lava

Record Breakers

BIGGEST VOLCANO
Mauna Kea in Hawaii is a massive volcano, 4,446 ft (1,355 m) taller than Mount Everest, but much of it is under the sea.

BIGGEST EARTHQUAKE
In 1960, an earthquake of 9.5 on the Richter scale was recorded in Chile. It caused tsunamis that reached Japan.

MOST DEVASTATING EARTHQUAKE
In 1556, an earthquake of magnitude 8.3 killed 800,000 people in Shansi, China.

HIGHEST TSUNAMI WAVE
The highest tsunami wave on record struck Ishigaki in Japan in 1971. The monstrous wave was 280 ft (85 m) high.

LARGEST FAULT SLIP
The largest ever fault slip was the main cause behind the 2011 tsunami in Japan. The fault in the floor of the North Pacific Ocean slipped by 165 ft (50 m).

Timeline

The timeline below includes just some of the major volcanic eruptions and earthquakes of the past four thousand years. We have most information about events in living memory or from records in recent history, but volcanologists can look much further back in time by studying the features of the Earth's surface.

Gas, dust, and rock explode from Mount St. Helens, 1980

c.1620 BCE Santorini, Greece

Violent eruptions buried the island of Santorini under 100 ft (30 m) of pumice.

79 CE Vesuvius, Italy

A burning cloud of volcanic ash engulfed the Roman towns of Pompeii and Herculaneum, killing thousands.

1755 Lisbon, Portugal

A earthquake measuring 8.5 on the Richter scale reduced the city to rubble.

1783 Skaftar fires, Iceland

A fissure (crack) 16 miles (27 km) long spewed out lava and poisonous gases.

Craters mark Skaftar fissure today

1815 Tambora, Indonesia

The biggest eruption ever recorded. Around 90,000 people were killed. Volcanic dust reduced levels of sunlight around the world.

1883 Krakatau, Indonesia

The force of the eruption left a crater 951 ft (290 m) deep in the ocean floor.

1902 Mount Pelée, Martinique

All but two of the entire population of St. Pierre were wiped out by the burning cloud of gas and dust. Around 30,000 people died.

1906 San Francisco

Two huge tremors hit the city, setting off fires that burned for many days.

1920 Xining, China

The entire province of Gansu was devastated by the earthquake, which killed more than 180,000 people.

1923 Tokyo, Japan

An earthquake of 8.3 on the Richter scale flattened 600,000 homes and knocked over stoves, which started a terrible firestorm.

A watch stopped by the eruption of Mount Pelée, 1902

1943 Paricutin, Mexico

Lava flowed from a crack that appeared in a farmer's field. By 1952, the cone stood 1,732 ft (528 m) tall.

1963 Surtsey, Iceland

Undersea volcanic explosions created a new island off the southwest coast of Iceland.

1963 Skopje, Yugoslavia

A violent earthquake left three-quarters of the town of Skopje homeless. At least 1,000 people were killed.

The ruins of San Francisco, 1906

Cinders engulf Vestmannaeyjar, Iceland

1973 Heimaey, Iceland

Eldfell volcano erupted after 5,000 years of dormancy. Molten lava engulfed one-third of the town of Vestmannaeyjar on the Icelandic island of Heimaey.

1976 Tangshan, China

The most disastrous earthquake in modern times. A tremor of 8.3 on the Richter scale killed over 240,000 people.

1980 Mount St. Helens, US

The eruption of Mount St. Helens devastated vast areas around the volcano.

1985 Mexico City, Mexico

Powerful tremors, measuring 8.1 on the Richter scale, shook Mexico City for three minutes. One million people were left homeless.

1985 Nevado del Ruiz, Colombia

The eruption of the Ruiz volcano caused a massive mudflow that engulfed the town of Armero 37 miles (60 km) away.

1991 Kilauea, Hawaii

Kilauea volcano suddenly produced large quantities of lava that buried 8 miles (13 km) of road and 181 homes.

1991 Pinatubo, Philippines

The most violent volcanic eruption of the twentieth century. Around 42,000 homes destroyed.

1994 Los Angeles

The earthquake destroyed nine highways and 11,000 buildings in 30 seconds.

1995 Kobe, Japan

The most powerful earthquake to hit a modern city, measuring 7.2 on the Richter scale.

1996 Grimsvotn, Iceland

A 2.5-mile- (4-km-) long fissure appeared in the side of the Grimsvotn volcano. Lava melting the glacier ice also damaged roads, pipelines, and power cables.

1998 New Guinea

A violent offshore earthquake caused a 33-ft- (10-m-) high tsunami, which swept 1.2 miles (2 km) inland. Around 4,500 people died.

2002 Democratic Republic of Congo

About half a million people were forced to leave their homes when rivers of lava flowed from Mount Nyiragongo. The lava destroyed two-fifths of the town.

2004 Sumatra-Andaman, Indian Ocean

An undersea earthquake triggered a series of tsunamis, killing around 187,000 people.

The destruction of the expressway, Kobe, Japan

2005 Pakistan

Also known as the Kashmir earthquake, this violent quake, measuring 7.6 on the Richter scale, killed around 73,000 people and left 33 million homeless.

2010 Haiti

A devastating 7.3 magnitude earthquake struck Haiti in January 2010. More than 220,000 people died.

2010 Iceland

In March 2010, Eyjafjallajökull volcano in Iceland erupted and disrupted air traffic across Europe for several weeks. About 45,000 passengers were affected.

2011 Japan

A 9.0 magnitude earthquake and tsunami struck Japan in March 2011. About 18,000 people lost their lives.

Eyjafjallajökull volcano, Iceland

Find out more

Volcanoes are unpredictable and can be extremely dangerous. However, there are volcanic parks all over the world where you can see volcanic features safely. There are also websites where you can find news of the latest eruptions and even watch volcanic activity live.

Yellowstone Park, US
These tourists are walking through the Norris geyser basin in Yellowstone National Park, Wyoming. Yellowstone lies on a volcanic hot spot and contains volcanic features such as geysers and fumaroles.

The story of an eruption

The remains of the cities of Pompeii and Herculaneum in Italy (pp. 26–32) give visitors an insight into both volcanoes and life in Roman times. Both cities were destroyed when Vesuvius erupted in 79 CE, but the volcano is still active—it last erupted in 1944. Visitors can climb up and look into the crater of the volcano.

The ruins of Pompeii lying in the shadow of Vesuvius

Bodies of ancient Romans suffocated by the poisonous gases were preserved in the volcanic ash

PLACES TO VISIT

MOUNT ST. HELENS NATIONAL VOLCANIC MONUMENT, WASHINGTON
The monument was established for research, recreation, and education.

CAPULIN MOUNTAIN, NEW MEXICO
This is one of the few places in the world where you can walk into a volcano.

CRATERS OF THE MOON, IDAHO
Here is the largest basaltic, dominantly holocene lava field in the contiguous US.

NATIONAL PARK, HAWAII
Experience the heartbeat of a volcano.

Runny pahoehoe lava flowing over a cliff made up of layers of lava

Visiting volcanoes

There are national parks worldwide where visitors can see signs of volcanic activity, past and present. In Hawaii, visitors can drive to the rim of the active volcano, Kilauea, walk through a lava tube, and see an eruption from a safe distance.

Lava flow from Kilauea volcano in Hawaii

WATCHING THE EARTH

In the box below you will find the addresses of some websites with general background information on volcanology and links to lots of specific volcanoes. The Smithsonian Institution produces an online weekly report on volcanic activity worldwide.

Living with a volcano
These children are learning about Sakurajima volcano in Japan. It is one of the most active volcanoes in the world, erupting around 150 times a year. Sakurajima is monitored by a volcano observatory which collects data that helps predict volcanic activity.

Watching from space
This picture, taken by a Space Shuttle, shows thick clouds of ash and dust from the eruption of Kliuchevskoi volcano in Russia, in 1994. Volcanic ash clouds can cause pollution and affect climate. They are watched and measured by satellites.

Dangerous work
This volcanologist is checking gas samples inside the crater of Mount Erebus, Antarctica. It is dangerous work and several volcanologists have been killed by unexpected eruptions. There are lots of sites on the Internet where you can learn more about a volcanologist's work and find out how to become one.

USEFUL WEBSITES

- A general introduction to volcanoes:
  www.geo.mtu.edu/volcanoes
- Smithsonian Institution report on volcanic activity:
  www.volcano.si.edu
- List of top ten earthquakes and volcanoes:
  www.uwgb.edu/dutchs/PLATETEC/TOPTEN.HTM
- On how to build a volcano model:
  www.sciencebob.com/experiments/volcano.php

Glossary

AA Hawaiian word to describe thick lava that forms angular lumps when cool.

AFTERSHOCKS Smaller earth tremors that happen after an earthquake. These may occur weeks after the main tremor.

ASH AND DUST The smallest fragments of lava formed when a volcano explodes. Small pieces are called ash, and the powder-fine particles are known as dust.

BASALT Dark, fine-grained volcanic rock, formed by runny lavas. Basalt is the most common volcanic rock.

BLACK SMOKER A volcanic hot spring on the ocean floor that spits out black water rich in minerals.

BOMBS AND BLOCKS Large pieces of lava thrown out during a volcanic eruption. Bombs are slightly rounded, while blocks are more angular.

CALDERA A giant, bowl-shaped crater at the top of a volcano, formed when the summit collapses into the volcano's magma chamber.

CARBONIZE To turn to carbon. Objects that contain carbon will turn to carbon (or charcoal), rather than burn, when there is not enough oxygen available for them to burn in the usual way.

Carbonized walnuts from Pompeii

A red-hot flow of aa lava, Hawaii

CORE The center of the Earth, made up of dense metals, in particular, iron. The inner core is solid while the outer core is liquid metal.

CRATER Hollow dip formed when the cone of a volcano collapses inwards.

CRATER LAKE Lake formed when water fills the crater or caldera of a volcano. Also known as lava lake.

DORMANT The term used to describe a volcano that has not been active for more than several hundred years but was active within the last several thousand years.

EPICENTER The point on the Earth's surface, directly above the focus, or point of origin, of an earthquake.

EXTINCT The term used to describe a volcano that has not been active for more than several thousand years.

FAULT A fracture in rock where blocks of rock slide past each other.

FEEDER PIPE The long tube through which magma passes to reach the surface.

FISSURE A crack in the earth. A fissure eruption is one where runny lava flows from the crack.

FOCUS The point within the Earth's mantle from which an earthquake originates.

FUMAROLE A vent or opening in the Earth's surface that releases steam or gas.

A geyser in Iceland

GEOLOGY The study of the history and development of Earth's rocks. The people who study geology are geologists.

GEYSER A place where water that has been superheated by hot magma bursts up into the air.

HOT SPOT A place in the middle of a tectonic plate, rather than at the boundary, where columns of magma from the mantle rise up through the crust creating a volcano.

The crater of Mount Vesuvius, Italy

HYDROTHERMAL VENT A place where mineral-rich water heated by hot magma underground erupts onto the surface. Geysers, black smokers, and hot springs are all hydrothermal vents.

IGNEOUS ROCKS Rocks formed as hot magma and lava cools.

INTENSITY The term used to describe the severity of the shaking experienced during an earthquake. It is usually measured using the Modified Mercalli Intensity Scale.

LAPILLI Small fragments of lava, formed as the magma bursts out of a volcano.

LAVA Hot, molten rock that erupts from a volcano.

LAVA TUBE A tunnel of lava created when the surface of a lava flow cools and hardens to form a roof, while hot, molten lava continues to flow inside it.

MAGMA Hot, molten rock originating from within Earth.

MAGMA CHAMBER Area beneath a volcano where magma builds up before an eruption.

MAGNITUDE The term used to describe the severity or scale of an earthquake. This is measured in several ways, the most common of which is the Richter scale.

MANTLE The layer between the Earth's crust and its core. The mantle is 1,800 miles (2,900 km) thick.

MERCALLI SCALE The scale for measuring the intensity of an earthquake by observing its effects.

MID-OCEAN RIDGE A mountain ridge on the ocean floor formed where two tectonic plates meet.

MUDFLOW A fast-moving stream of mud, water, and often volcanic ash and pumice.

PAHOEHOE The Hawaiian term for hot, runny lava that flows quickly and, usually, in quite shallow flows.

PILLOW LAVA Rounded lava formations shaped when lava erupts gently underwater.

PLATE TECTONICS The theory that the Earth's surface is broken up into large slabs or plates that are moving constantly at the rate of about half an inch a year. Most volcanoes and earthquakes are found at the boundaries of these plates.

PUMICE Lightweight volcanic rock filled with holes formed by the bubbles of gas in the lava.

SEISMIC WAVES The vibrations, or shock waves, that radiate out from the focus of an earthquake.

Pumice

SEISMOGRAM The record produced by a seismograph, showing the pattern of shock waves from an earthquake.

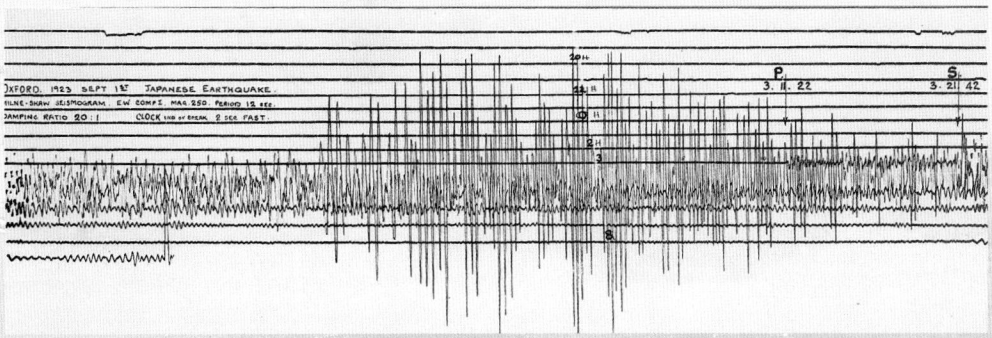

Seismogram of the 1923 Tokyo earthquake

Aa lava

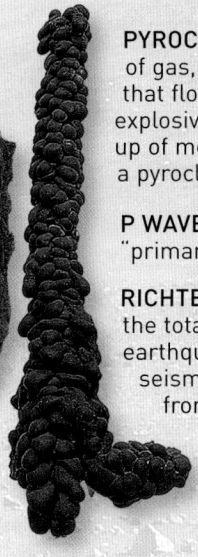

Pahoehoe lava

PYROCLASTIC FLOW A burning cloud of gas, dust, ash, rocks, and bombs that flows down the mountain after an explosive eruption. If the cloud is made up of more gas than ash, it is known as a pyroclastic surge.

P WAVES The fastest and first or "primary" waves of an earthquake.

RICHTER SCALE Scale for measuring the total energy released by earthquakes and recorded by seismographs. The scale ranges from 1 to 10, with 10 at the most severe end of the scale.

RING OF FIRE The area encircling the Pacific Ocean where most volcanic and earthquake activity occurs.

SEISMOMETER A machine for detecting earthquake shock waves. The machine that records the data is a seismograph.

SUBDUCTION ZONE The area where two tectonic plates meet and one plate is pushed down into the mantle, partly melting rocks. The resulting magma erupts at the surface through volcanoes.

S WAVES The slower, "secondary" waves of an earthquake.

TSUNAMI Fast-moving waves caused by earthquakes or volcanic eruption that displace the ocean floor and water.

VENT The opening through which a volcanic eruption occurs.

VOLCANOLOGIST A scientist who studies volcanoes.

Volcanologists collecting gas samples on Colima volcano, in Mexico

Index

A

aa flow 19, 40, 70
acid lake 21, 38
Africa 10, 20, 24, 50
aftershocks 46, 55, 59, 70
agates 38, 39
Alaska 7, 11, 35, 46
Aleutian Islands 11
Antarctica 11, 35, 69
Armenian earthquake 59
Armero, Colombia 56, 58, 67
ash 7, 14, 15, 16–17, 26, 28, 29, 30, 31, 34–35, 40–41, 57, 64, 69
Assisi, Italy 7
asthenosphere 13
Atlantic 11
atmosphere 14, 16, 34, 35
Augustine volcano Alaska 7
Australia 11, 35
avalanches 56, 57

BC

Barry, James 8
basalt 8, 70
black smokers 24–25, 70
Brazil 39
Britain 16
Bruillov, Karl 28
calderas 39, 44, 45, 70
California 61
Cameroon, Africa 20
Caribbean 32, 51
Cascade range, USA 14, 39
Caspian Sea 50
Catania, Sicily 7
Chile 46, 65
China 65, 66, 67
Ciparis, Auguste 33
Colombia 56, 58, 67
cone 16, 22, 40, 66
continental drift 10
core 8, 9, 70
craters 14, 22, 31, 36, 38, 53, 63, 66, 68, 70
Crete, Greece 39
crystals 25, 36, 37, 38, 39, 40
Cyprus 25

DEF

de Saint-Exupéry, Antoine 44
Democratic Republic of Congo 67
dormant volcanoes 6, 26, 36, 38–39, 45, 65, 70
dust 16, 20, 34
Earth 8, 9, 10, 12, 22, 44, 50, 62
England 54
epicenter 49, 50, 51, 70
Europe 7, 34, 47
extinct volcanoes 22, 44, 65, 70
Eyjafjallajökull, Iceland 67
Fabris, Pietro 31, 39
Faëroe Islands 38
faults 13, 61, 65, 70
Filomarino, Ascanio 53
Fiorelli, Giuseppe 28, 29
fire fountains 16, 18, 22
France 38
Fukushima, Japan 57
fumaroles 36–37, 70

GH

gabbro 25
Galápagos rift 25
gas 14, 16, 18, 19, 20–21, 26, 32, 34, 36, 38
gemstones 39
geysers 7, 36–37, 64, 68, 70
granite 8
Gray, Thomas 54
Gray-Milne seismograph 54
Greece 19, 39, 63, 66
Grimsvotn, Iceland 67
Guadeloupe 51
Guatemala 13
Haiti 59, 67
Halema'uma'u, Hawaii 22
Hamilton, Lord 21, 31, 39
Hasan Dag, Turkey 6
Hawaii 19, 22, 23, 40, 65, 67, 68
Heimaey, Iceland 65, 67
Herculaneum, Italy 11, 26, 30–31, 60, 68
Hokusai, Katsushika 6, 57
hot spots 11, 12, 22–23
hot springs 24, 25, 36, 37, 64, 68, 70
hydrothermal features 36–37, 71

IJK

Iceland 11, 12, 20, 22, 24, 34, 37, 38, 41, 64, 65, 66, 67, 68
India 11, 50
Indian Ocean 23, 35, 67
Indonesia 11, 20, 21, 35, 37, 64,
Iran 58
iron 9, 33
Italy 7, 11, 16, 18, 26–31, 35, 36, 40, 47, 48, 52, 53, 57, 62, 66, 68, 70
Japan 6, 7, 11, 34, 37, 38, 42, 49, 54, 56, 57, 60, 61, 63, 64, 66, 65, 67, 69
Java, Indonesia 20, 21, 37, 64
Kamchatka, Siberia 11, 21
Kawah Idjen, Java 20, 21
Kilauea volcano, Hawaii 22, 23, 40, 65, 67, 68
Kimberley, South Africa 39
Kircher, Athanasius 8
Kliuchevskoi 69
Kobe, Japan 67
Krafft, Katia and Maurice 42, 43
Kyoto, Japan 11

LM

Lacroix, Alfred 32
Lake Nyos, Cameroon 20
landslides 51, 56
lapilli 16, 29, 71
lava 7, 8, 18–19, 22–23, 31, 43, 65, 66, 67, 71
aa 19, 40
pahoehoe 19, 23, 40, 68, 71
pyroclastic 14, 16, 26, 29, 30, 31, 32, 64, 71
Le Puy, France 38
Lice, Turkey 51
Lisbon, Portugal 47, 66
lithosphere 9, 13
Loihi volcano, Hawaii 22
Los Angeles 67
Macedonia 67
Madagascar 35
magma 8–9, 12, 13, 14, 20, 38, 47, 70
mantle 8, 9, 12, 13, 22, 39, 71
Mars 44
Mauna Loa volcano, Hawaii 22, 65
Mercalli, Guiseppe 48
meteorites 9, 55
Mexico 35, 62, 65, 66, 67, 71
mid-ocean ridges 10, 11, 12, 24–25, 71
Milne, John 54
minerals 19, 25, 37, 38
Modified Mercalli Scale 48–49
Moon 44, 55
Mount El Chichón, Mexico 35
Mount Erebus, Antarctica 11, 69
Mount Etna, Sicily 7, 8, 18, 68
Mount Fujiyama, Japan 6, 57, 63
Mount Katmai, Alaska 35
Mount Kea, Hawaii 65
Mount Krakatau, Indonesia 35, 57, 64, 66
Mount Pelée, Martinique 32, 66
Mount Pinatubo, Philippines 17, 35, 56, 64, 67
Mount Rainier 39
Mount St. Helens 14, 15, 34, 35, 64, 67
Mount Tambora, Indonesia 35, 64, 66
Mount Unzen, Japan 42
Mount Vesuvius, Italy 11, 21, 26–31, 35, 40, 41, 53, 55, 60, 62, 63, 66, 68, 70
mud 38, 56, 58, 67, 70

NO

Naples Italy, 16, 21, 26, 31, 57, 62
New Guinea 67
New Zealand 65
Nicaragua 62
Old Faithful geyser 7, 37
ozone layer, 35

PQ

Pacific 10, 11, 22, 24,57, 65
pahoehoe lava 19, 23, 40, 68, 71
Pakistan 67
Palmieri, Luigi 52, 53
Paricutin, Mexico 65, 66
Parkfield, California 61
Peru 57
Philippines 17, 35, 56, 64, 67
pillow lava 24–25, 71
Piton de la Fournaise volcano, Réunion 23, 43, 47
Pliny 26, 27
plume 45
Pointe-à-Pitre, Guadeloupe 51
Pompeii, Italy 11, 16, 26–29, 41, 47, 61, 66, 68, 70
Popocatépetl, Mexico 62
Pozzuoli, Italy 57
pumice 16, 21, 28, 30, 35, 56, 66, 70
pyroclastics 14, 16, 26, 29, 30, 31, 32, 64, 71

RS

Red Sea 24, 39
Réunion island 11, 23, 43, 47
Richter, Charles F 49
Richter scale 47, 48–49, 65, 66, 67, 71
Ring of Fire 10, 11, 71
Ruiz, Colombia 56, 67
Russia 69
Sakurajima 69
St. John's Island, Red Sea 39
St. Pierre, Martinique 32, 33, 66
San Andreas fault 13, 61
San Francisco 7, 46, 57, 60, 66
Santorini, Greece 19, 39, 66
Scupi, Yugoslavia 46
seismography 48, 49, 50, 52–55
Shirane volcano, Japan 38
shock waves 50, 51, 55
Siberia 21
Sicily 7, 18, 36
Skaftar, Iceland 24, 34, 66
Skopje, Yugoslavia 46, 66
sniffer dogs 59
Solfatara, Italy 26, 36, 37, 39
South Africa 39
South America 10, 56
spreading ridges 10, 11, 12, 24–25
subduction zones 12, 13, 71
sulfur 20, 31, 35, 36, 37
Sumatra 64, 67
Surtsey island 20, 41, 66

TUV

Tangshan, China 67
tectonic plates 10–13, 22, 24, 25
thermal image camera 58
thermocouple 36, 43
tidal waves, *see* tsunamis
Tokyo, Japan 54, 60, 66
Tolbachik volcano, Siberia 21
trapped person detector 59
tremors 46, 47, 52, 53, 55, 66, 67
tsunamis 47, 56, 57, 63, 64, 65, 67, 71
Turkey 6, 51
Twain, Mark 29
United States 7, 11, 14–15, 35, 37, 46, 57, 60, 61, 65, 66, 67, 68, 69
Valparaiso, Chile 46
vent 20, 36, 37, 71
Verne, Jules 8
Venus 44
volcanologist 20, 21, 32, 42–43, 48, 66, 69, 71
Voltaire 47
vulcanization 36

WXYZ

Wegener, Alfred 10
Wiechert, Emil 55
Wright, Frank Lloyd 60
Xining, China 66
Yugoslavia 46, 66
Zhang Heng 52

Acknowledgments

Dorling Kindersley would like to thank: John Lepine & Jane Insley of the Science Museum, London; Robert Symes, Colin Keates & Tim Parmenter of the Natural History Museum, London; the staff at the Museo Archeologico di Napoli; Giuseppe Luongo, Luigi Iadicicco & Vincenzo D' Errico at the Vesuvius Observatory for help in photographing the instruments on pp. 49, 53, & 55; Paul Arthur; Paul Cole; Lina Ferrante at Pompeii; Dott. Angarano at Solfatara; Carlo Illario at Herculaneum; Roger Musson of the British Geological Survey; Joe Cann; Tina Chambers for extra photography; Gin von Noorden & Helena Spiteri for editorial assistance; Céline Carez for research & development; Wilfred Wood & Earl Neish for design assistance; Jane Parker for the index; Stewart J. Wild for proofreading; Carol Davis for art-editing the jacket; Neville Graham, Sue Nicholson, & Susan St. Louis for the wallchart.

Illustrations: John Woodcock

Maps: Sallie Alane Reason

Models: David Donkin (pp. 8–9, 50–51) & Edward Laurence Associates (pp. 12–13)

For this relaunch edition, the publisher would also like to thank: Hazel Beynon for text editing, and Carron Brown for proofreading.

The Publishers would like to thank the following for their kind permission to reproduce their photographs:

a-above; b-below; c-centre; l-left; r-right; t-top
Ancient Art & Architecture Collection: 47t. **Art Directors Photo Library:** 47tc, 49tc. **B.F.I.:** 46cr, 57cr. **Bridgeman Art Library:** 6tl & c. **Musee des Beaux-Arts, Lille:** 44tl. **British Museum:** 27tr & c. **Herge/Casterman:** 20tl. **Dr Joe Cann, University of Leeds:** 25bc. **Jean-Loup Charmet:** 27bl, 31tl, 46bl, 51tl. **Circus World Museum, Baraboo, Wisconsin:** 32br. **Corbis:** Bettmann 67tl; Danny Lehman 65cr; Vittoriano Rastelli 70tc; Roger Ressmeyer 71br; Michael S. Yamashita / National Geographic Society (57cl). **Eric Crichton:** 41tr, 41bl. **Culver Pictures Inc:** 60br. **DK Images:** Satellite Imagemap © 1996–2003 Planetary Visions 9c. **Dreamstime.com:** Photographerlondon (67b). **Earthquake Research Institute, University of Tokyo:** 63cr. **Edimedia/Russian Museum, Leningrad:** 28cl. **E.T. Archive:** 49c, 58tr, 62tl. **Mary Evans Picture Library:** 8tc, 16tl, 26tl, 27br, 28c, 29cr, 46tl, 64cr, 66br. **Le Figaro Magazine/Philippe Bourseiller:** 19t, 19cl 19bl, 19br, 35tr. **Fiorepress:** 49br. **Gallimard:** 44tr. **G.S.F.:** 13tl, 14bl; /Frank Fitch: 20c. **John Guest c.NASA:** 44bl. **Robert Harding Picture Library:** 12tl, 14tr, 15cr 17tr, 17cr, 20tr, 21br, 63br, 24tl, 38br, 39br, 40tr, 42c, 43br, 48br, 49bl, 51tr, 60lc, 62bl, 62–63c, Explorer 66bl, Christian Kober (59bl). **Bruce C. Heezen & Marie Tharp, 1977/c.Marie Tharp:** 11c. **Historical Pictures Service, Inc.:** 10cr. **Michael Holford:** 22tr. **Illustrated London News:** 60bl. **ImageState:** 68bc. **Katz Pictures:** Alberto Garcia/Saba 64b. **Frank Lane Picture Agency:** 23rct, 23c. **Frank Lane Picture Agency/S.Jonasson:** 41tc, 49cr. **Archive Larousse-Giraudon:** 32cl. **London Fire Brigade/LFCDA:** 58bl. **Mansell Collection:** 31tr. **NASA:** 24bc, 55cr, 68–69. **Natural History Museum:** 34tl. **National Maritime Museum:** 8tl. **Orion Press:** 7tr, 61bl. **Oxford Scientific Films/ Colin Monteath:** 69br; /NASA: 69cl; /Kim Westerkov: 11bl; 15tl. Planet Earth Pictures/ Franz J.Camenzind: 7cr; /D.Weisel: 17br; /James D. Watt: 23rcb; /Robert Hessler: 25tr, 25lc. **Popperfoto:** 6b, 11tr, 54tl. **R.C.S. Rizzoli:** 48lc. **Rex Features:** 67tr. **Gary Rosenquist:** 14tl, 14br, 15tr, 15br. **Scala:** 7c, 49bl(inset); /Louvre: 63tr. **Science Photo Library/Earth Sattelite Corp.:** 7tl; /Peter Menzel: 7br, 20br, 46cl, 65bl; /David Parker: 13tr, 61tl, 61tr, 65tc; /Ray Fairbanks: 18c; /Inst Oceanographic Sciences: 24c; /Matthew Shipp: 24bl; /NASA: 35c, 43cr, 44cr, 44c, 44–45b; /U.S.G.S.: 45tr; /Peter Ryan: 55tr; /David Weintraub 66t. **Frank Spooner Pictures:** 8cl, 16cr, 17tl, 22bl, 23tr, 23br, 35tc, 42cl, 47cl, 49cl, 56tl, 56c, 56bl, 57bl, 58tl, 59tr, 59br, 61lcb; /Nigel Hicks 69tr. **Syndication International:** 31cr; /Inst. **Geological Science:** 32tc, 35br, 41tl, 47br; /Daily Mirror: 54tr, 57tr. **Susanna van Rose:** 39bl. **Woods Hole Oceanographic Institute/Rod Catanach:** 24br; /Dudley Foster: 25bl; /J. Frederick Grassle: 25tc; /Robert Hessler: 25tl. **ZEFA:** 9tl, 21t, 34bl, 45br, 57br.

All other images © Dorling Kindersley.
For further information see:
www.dkimages.com